One Pot & Casseroles

One Pot & Casseroles

Cooking Your Way to Good Living

This edition published by Parragon Books Ltd in 2016
LOVE FOOD is an imprint of Parragon Books Ltd

Parragon Books Ltd
Chartist House
15–17 Trim Street
Bath BA1 1HA, UK
www.parragon.com/lovefood

ISBN 978-1-4748-4997-5

Printed in China

Internal design by Ignition
Additional photography by Mike Cooper
Additional food styling by Lincoln Jefferson

Notes for the Reader

- This book uses both metric and imperial measurements. Follow the same units of measurement throughout; do not mix metric and imperial. All spoon measurements are level: teaspoons are assumed to be 5 ml, and tablespoons are assumed to be 15 ml. Unless otherwise stated, milk is assumed to be full fat, eggs and individual fruits and vegetables are medium, pepper is freshly ground black pepper and salt is table salt. A pinch of salt is calculated as 1/16 of a teaspoon. Unless otherwise stated, all root vegetables should be peeled prior to using.

- The times given are an approximate guide only. Preparation times differ according to the techniques used by different people and the cooking times may also vary from those given.

- For best results, use a food thermometer when cooking meat. Check the latest government guidelines for current advice.

These days most of us lead action-packed lives, either at work or as a busy parent, or both. Time-consuming meal preparation, let alone clearing up afterwards, just doesn't fit in very easily. Yet most of us care about health and want to eat nutritious home-cooked food.

As the recipes in the book demonstrate, this no-frills way of cooking is the ultimate in terms of convenience since everything is ready at the same time. It's the ideal food for solitary suppers or for feeding a crowd. Just put the pot on the table and tuck in.

GETTING STARTED
Before you start to cook:
• Read the recipe all the way through, then plan the sequence according to what needs soaking, chopping, precooking, etc.
• Have the right tools and cookware to hand
• Make sure knives are sharp
• Wash fresh vegetables, fruits and herbs
• Assemble all the ingredients then measure or weigh them as necessary
• Complete any pre-preparation such as chopping or grating
• Have the prepared ingredients lined up in bowls, ready to add to the pot at the correct time
• Clear up as you go along

USEFUL UTENSILS
As well as basics such as knives and chopping boards, there are a number of additional utensils that make one pot cooking easier and safer.
• Though you can happily leave the pot to simmer while you get on with something else, it's still important to keep track of temperature and time. Thermometers are essential for food safety, and a timer with a loud ring is invaluable for reminding you when the dish needs your attention. You'll also need spoons and spatulas for stirring, and tools for turning and lifting ingredients that are precooked in stages before they go into the pot. A sturdy long-handled fork or multipronged meat lifter are handy for large pieces of meat, while stainless steel spring-action tongs allow you to clasp smaller pieces of food

securely. A perforated shallow skimmer is useful for removing froth and scum from the surface of stews.
• Although one pot recipes are infinitely flexible, it's worth investing in proper measuring spoons and jugs, as well as kitchen scales, especially if you are new to cooking. Once you gain experience and confidence, it's fine to add a pinch of this and a handful of that.
• The joy of one pot meals is that they can be brought straight from oven to table.

COOKWARE
For most of the recipes in this book, a few heavy-based saucepans and casseroles in varying sizes with tight-fitting lids make up the basic equipment. You'll also need a high-sided frying pan, a wok, good-quality roasting tins that won't warp or twist, and some shallow baking dishes for gratins and crumbles.

FRESH PRODUCE
Wholesome fresh vegetables, meat, poultry and fish add valuable nutrients to one pot meals, as well as colour, texture and appetizing flavours.

Vegetables
One of the most important sources of vitamins, minerals and fibre, vegetables are packed with carotenoids (the plant form of vitamin A), vitamin C and vitamin E, which collectively protect against heart disease and some cancers.

Meat and poultry
Meat and poultry provide high quality protein, important minerals such as iron and zinc, and B vitamins, needed to release energy from food. Meat tends to be high in fat, so if you're trying to cut down, trim off any excess or choose lean cuts.

Fish and seafood
Dense-fleshed fish and seafood make marvellous one pot meals. They provide protein and essential minerals, while oily fish such as tuna are a unique source of omega-3 fatty acids that protect against heart disease and feed the brain.

Fresh herbs
A generous sprinkling of fresh herbs added at the end of cooking will provide delightful fragrance and colour to one pot meals.

Beef Stock
Makes 1.7 litres/3 pints

1 kg/2 lb 4 oz beef marrow bones, sawn into
7.5-cm/3-inch pieces
650 g/1 lb 7 oz stewing beef in a single piece
2.8 litres/5 pints water
4 cloves
2 onions, halved
2 celery sticks, roughly chopped
8 peppercorns
1 bouquet garni

• Put the bones in a large, heavy-based saucepan
and put the stewing beef on top. Pour in the water
and bring to the boil over a low heat. Skim off the
scum that rises to the surface.
• Press a clove into each onion half and add to
the pan with the celery, peppercorns and bouquet
garni. Partially cover and simmer gently for 3 hours.
Remove the stewing beef from the pan, partially
re-cover and simmer for a further hour.
• Remove the pan from the heat and leave to cool.
Strain the stock into a bowl, cover with clingfilm
and chill in the refrigerator for at least 1 hour and
preferably overnight.
• Remove and discard the layer of fat that has set
on the surface. Use immediately or freeze for up to
6 months.

Chicken Stock
Makes 2.5 litres/4½ pints

1.3 kg/3 lb chicken wings and necks
2 onions, cut into wedges
4 litres/7 pints water
2 carrots, roughly chopped
2 celery sticks, roughly chopped
10 fresh parsley sprigs
4 fresh thyme sprigs
2 bay leaves
10 black peppercorns

• Place the chicken and onions in a large, heavy-
based saucepan and cook over a low heat, stirring
frequently, until browned all over.
• Pour in the water and stir well, scraping up any
sediment from the base of the pan. Bring to the boil
and skim off the scum that rises to the surface.
• Add the carrots, celery, parsley, thyme, bay leaves
and peppercorns, partially cover the pan and
simmer gently, stirring occasionally, for 3 hours.
• Remove the pan from the heat and leave to cool.
Strain the stock into a bowl, cover with clingfilm
and chill in the refrigerator for at least 1 hour and
preferably overnight.

• Remove and discard the layer of fat that has set
on the surface. Use immediately or freeze for up to
6 months.

Fish Stock
Makes 1.3 litres/2¼ pints

650 g/1 lb 7 oz white fish heads, bones
  and trimmings
1 onion, sliced
2 celery sticks, chopped
1 carrot, sliced
1 bay leaf
4 fresh parsley sprigs
4 black peppercorns
½ lemon, sliced
125 ml/4 fl oz dry white wine
1.3 litres/2¼ pints water

• Cut out and discard the gills from the fish heads,
then rinse the heads, bones and trimmings. Place
them in a large, heavy-based saucepan.
• Add all the remaining ingredients. Bring to the boil
and skim off the scum that rises to the surface. Lower
the heat, partially cover and simmer gently for
25 minutes.
• Remove the pan from the heat and leave to cool.
Strain the stock into a bowl, without pressing down
on the contents of the colander.
• Use immediately or freeze for up to 3 months.

Vegetable Stock
Makes 2 litres/3½ pints

2 tbsp sunflower or corn oil
115 g/4 oz onions, finely chopped
115 g/4 oz leeks, finely chopped
115 g/4 oz carrots, finely chopped
4 celery sticks, finely chopped
85 g/3 oz fennel, finely chopped
85 g/3 oz tomatoes, finely chopped
2.25 litres/4 pints water
1 bouquet garni

• Heat the oil in a large, heavy-based saucepan.
Add the onions and leeks and cook over a low heat,
stirring occasionally, for 5 minutes, until softened.
• Add the carrots, celery, fennel and tomatoes, cover
and cook, stirring occasionally, for 10 minutes. Pour
in the water, add the bouquet garni and bring to
the boil. Lower the heat and simmer for 20 minutes.
• Remove the pan from the heat and leave to cool.
Strain the stock into a bowl. Use immediately or
freeze for up to 3 months.

Soups

SERVES 6

2 carrots, sliced
1 onion, diced
1 garlic clove, crushed
350 g/12 oz new
 potatoes, diced
2 celery sticks, sliced
115 g/4 oz closed-cup
 mushrooms, quartered

400 g/14 oz canned
 chopped tomatoes in
 tomato juice
600 ml/1 pint vegetable
 stock
1 bay leaf
1 tsp dried mixed herbs
 or 1 tbsp chopped
 fresh mixed herbs

85 g/3 oz sweetcorn
 kernels, frozen or
 canned, drained
55 g/2 oz green
 cabbage, shredded
pepper
crusty wholemeal or
 white bread rolls,
 to serve

Chunky Vegetable Soup

Put the carrots, onion, garlic, potatoes, celery, mushrooms, tomatoes and stock into a large saucepan. Stir in the bay leaf and herbs. Bring to the boil, then reduce the heat, cover and simmer for 25 minutes.

Add the sweetcorn and cabbage and return to the boil. Reduce the heat, cover and simmer for 5 minutes, or until the vegetables are tender. Remove and discard the bay leaf. Season to taste with pepper.

Ladle into warmed bowls and serve immediately with crusty bread rolls.

SERVES 4

2 tbsp olive oil
1 onion, chopped
1 garlic clove, chopped
1 tbsp chopped fresh
  ginger

1 small red chilli,
  deseeded and finely
  chopped
2 tbsp chopped fresh
  coriander
1 bay leaf

1 kg/2 lb 4 oz pumpkin,
  peeled, deseeded and
  diced
600 ml/1 pint vegetable
  stock
salt and pepper
single cream, to garnish

Spiced Pumpkin Soup

Heat the oil in a saucepan over a medium heat. Add the onion and garlic and
cook, stirring, for about 4 minutes, until slightly softened. Add the ginger, chilli,
coriander, bay leaf and pumpkin and cook for another 3 minutes.

Pour in the stock and bring to the boil. Using a slotted spoon, skim any scum from
the surface. Reduce the heat and simmer gently, stirring occasionally, for about
25 minutes, or until the pumpkin is tender. Remove from the heat, discard the bay
leaf and leave to cool a little.

Transfer the soup to a food processor or blender and process until smooth
(you may have to do this in batches). Return the mixture to the rinsed-out pan and
season to taste with salt and pepper. Reheat gently, stirring. Remove from the heat,
pour into 4 warmed soup bowls, garnish each one with a swirl of cream and serve.

SERVES 4

3 tbsp olive oil
2 onions, chopped
2 garlic cloves, chopped
2 large red peppers, deseeded and chopped

500 g/1 lb 2 oz ripe tomatoes, chopped
100 g/3½ oz red split lentils
600 ml/1 pint vegetable stock, plus extra to thin (optional)

1 tbsp red wine vinegar
salt and pepper
2 spring onions, sliced, to garnish

Tomato, Lentil & Red Pepper Soup

Heat the oil in a large frying pan over a medium–high heat, add the onions and cook, stirring, for 5 minutes, or until softened but not browned. Add the garlic and red peppers and cook, stirring, for 5 minutes, or until the red peppers are softened.

Add the tomatoes, lentils and stock and bring to a simmer. Reduce the heat to low, cover and simmer gently for 25 minutes, or until the lentils are tender. Stir in the vinegar and season to taste with salt and pepper.

Leave to cool slightly, then transfer the soup to a blender or food processor and blend for 1 minute, or until smooth. Return to the frying pan and reheat, stirring in a little hot water or stock if the soup seems a little too thick.

Ladle into warmed bowls, garnish with the spring onions and serve.

SERVES 4

2 tbsp olive oil
1 onion, chopped
2 celery sticks, chopped
1 large carrot, roughly
    chopped
1 large or 2 small sweet
    potatoes, peeled and
    chopped

400 g/14 oz canned
    butter beans or
    cannellini beans,
    drained and rinsed
1 litre/1¾ pints vegetable
    stock
salt and pepper

1 large handful fresh
    coriander leaves,
    to garnish
2 tbsp freshly grated
    Parmesan cheese,
    to serve

Sweet Potato & Butter Bean Soup

Heat the oil in a large saucepan over a medium heat, add the onion, celery and carrot and cook, stirring frequently, for 8–10 minutes, or until softened. Add the sweet potatoes and beans and cook, stirring, for 1 minute.

Add the stock, stir thoroughly and bring to a simmer. Season to taste with salt and pepper. Cover, reduce the heat and cook for 25–30 minutes, or until all the vegetables are tender.

Leave to cool slightly, then transfer one third of the soup to a blender or food processor and blend until smooth. Return to the saucepan and mix in well. Check the seasoning and reheat.

Ladle into warmed bowls, garnish with the coriander, top with Parmesan cheese and serve.

SERVES 6

225 g/8 oz dried red split lentils
1 red onion, diced
2 large carrots, sliced

1 celery stick, sliced
1 parsnip, diced
1 garlic clove, crushed
1.2 litres/2 pints vegetable stock

2 tsp paprika
pepper
1 tbsp snipped fresh chives, to garnish

Red Lentil Soup

Put the lentils, onion, vegetables, garlic, stock and paprika into a large saucepan. Bring to the boil and boil rapidly for 10 minutes. Reduce the heat, cover and simmer for 20 minutes, or until the lentils and vegetables are tender.

Leave the soup to cool slightly, then purée in small batches in a food processor or blender. Process until the mixture is smooth.

Return the soup to the saucepan and heat through thoroughly. Season to taste with pepper.

Ladle the soup into warmed bowls, garnish with the snipped chives and serve.

SERVES 4

2 tbsp groundnut oil
450 g/1 lb stewing beef, in 1 piece
2 celery sticks, chopped
1 medium onion, chopped
2 tsp finely chopped fresh ginger
55 g/2 oz pearl barley

2 star anise
½ cinnamon stick
2 cloves
1 tsp chipotle chilli powder, or to taste
1 litre/1¾ pints beef stock
1.2 litres/2 pints water
2 tbsp Thai fish sauce, or to taste

1 tbsp fresh lime juice, or to taste
1 tbsp chopped fresh coriander
1 tbsp chopped fresh mint
2 spring onions, finely chopped

Beef + Barley Soup

In a large saucepan, heat the oil over a medium–high heat. Add the beef and cook for about 10 minutes, until browned on all sides. Using a slotted spoon, remove the beef from the pan and place in a bowl. Reduce the heat to medium, add the celery, onion, ginger, and pearl barley and sauté for about 10 minutes, until the onion is softened and golden. Add the star anise, cinnamon stick, cloves and chipotle chilli powder and cook for about 2 minutes, until aromatic.

Return the beef to the pan, add the beef stock, water and fish sauce, and bring to the boil. Reduce the heat and simmer, uncovered, for about 1–1½ hours, or until the beef is tender. Using a slotted spoon, remove the beef from the pan. Cool slightly, then shred the meat. Return the beef to the pan and cook to heat through. Add the lime juice. Taste and add additional fish sauce or lime juice, if needed. Stir in the coriander, mint and spring onions. Ladle into warmed bowls and serve.

SERVES 4

2 tbsp vegetable oil
1 large onion, finely
   chopped
2 garlic cloves, finely
   chopped
1 green pepper,
   deseeded and sliced

2 carrots, sliced
400 g/14 oz canned
   black-eyed beans
225 g/8 oz fresh beef
   mince
1 tsp each ground
   cumin, chilli powder
   and paprika

¼ cabbage, sliced
225 g/8 oz tomatoes,
   peeled and chopped
600 ml/1 pint beef stock
salt and pepper

Beef + Bean Soup

Heat the oil in a large saucepan over a medium heat. Add the onion and garlic and cook, stirring frequently, for 3 minutes, or until softened. Add the green pepper and carrots and cook for a further 5 minutes.

Meanwhile, drain the beans, reserving the liquid from the can. Place two thirds of the beans, reserving the remainder, in a food processor or blender with the bean liquid and process until smooth.

Add the beef to the saucepan and cook, stirring constantly, to break up any lumps, until well browned. Add the spices and cook, stirring, for 2 minutes. Add the cabbage, tomatoes, stock and puréed beans and season to taste with salt and pepper. Bring to the boil, then reduce the heat, cover and simmer for 15 minutes, or until the vegetables are tender.

Stir in the reserved beans, cover and simmer for a further 5 minutes. Ladle the soup into warmed soup bowls and serve.

SERVES 4

150 g/5½ oz lean lamb
50 g/1¾ oz rice
850 ml/1½ pints lamb or
  vegetable stock

1 leek, sliced
1 garlic clove, thinly
  sliced
2 tsp light soy sauce

1 tsp rice wine vinegar
1 medium open-cap
  mushroom, thinly sliced
salt

Lamb + Rice Soup

Using a sharp knife, trim any fat from the lamb and cut the meat into thin strips. Set aside until required.

Bring a large pan of lightly salted water to the boil and add the rice. Bring back to the boil, stir once, reduce the heat and cook for 10–15 minutes, until tender. Drain the cooked rice, rinse under cold running water, drain again and set aside.

Put the lamb stock in a large saucepan and bring to the boil. Add the lamb strips, leek, garlic, soy sauce and rice wine vinegar, reduce the heat, cover and simmer for 10 minutes, or until the lamb is tender and cooked through.

Add the mushroom slices and cooked rice to the saucepan and cook for a further 2–3 minutes, or until the mushroom is completely cooked through.

Ladle the soup into warmed bowls and serve immediately.

SERVES 4-6

1-2 tbsp olive oil
450 g/1 lb boneless lamb, cut into cubes
1 onion, finely chopped
2-3 garlic cloves, crushed
1.2 litres/2 pints water
400 g/14 oz canned chopped tomatoes
1 bay leaf

½ tsp each dried thyme and dried oregano
⅛ tsp ground cinnamon
¼ tsp each cumin and turmeric
1 tsp harissa, or more to taste
400 g/14 oz canned chickpeas, rinsed and drained

1 carrot, diced
1 potato, diced
1 courgette, quartered lengthways and sliced
100 g/3½ oz fresh or defrosted frozen green peas
sprigs of fresh mint or coriander, to garnish

Spicy Lamb & Chickpea Soup

Heat 1 tablespoon of the oil in a large saucepan over a medium-high heat. Add the lamb, in batches if necessary to avoid crowding the pan, and cook until evenly browned on all sides, adding a little more oil if needed. Remove the meat with a slotted spoon when browned.

Reduce the heat and add the onion and garlic to the pan. Cook, stirring frequently, for 1-2 minutes.

Add the water and return all the meat to the pan. Bring just to the boil and skim off any scum that rises to the surface. Reduce the heat and stir in the tomatoes, bay leaf, thyme, oregano, cinnamon, cumin, turmeric and harissa. Simmer for about 1 hour, or until the meat is very tender. Remove and discard the bay leaf.

Stir in the chickpeas, carrot and potato and simmer for 15 minutes. Add the courgette and peas and continue simmering for 15-20 minutes, or until all the vegetables are tender.

Taste and add more harissa, if desired. Ladle the soup into warmed bowls and garnish with mint or coriander.

SERVES 4

1 tbsp chilli oil
1 garlic clove, chopped
3 spring onions, sliced
1 red pepper, deseeded
  and finely sliced
2 tbsp cornflour
1 litre/1¾ pints vegetable
  stock
1 tbsp soy sauce

2 tbsp rice wine or dry
  sherry
150 g/5½ oz pork fillet,
  sliced
1 tbsp finely chopped
  lemon grass
1 small red chilli,
  deseeded and finely
  chopped

1 tbsp grated fresh ginger
115 g/4 oz fine egg
  noodles
200 g/7 oz canned water
  chestnuts, drained and
  sliced
salt and pepper

Pork + Vegetable Broth

Heat the oil in a large saucepan. Add the garlic and spring onions and cook over a medium heat, stirring, for 3 minutes, until slightly softened. Add the red pepper and cook for a further 5 minutes, stirring.

In a bowl, mix the cornflour with enough of the stock to make a smooth paste, then stir it into the pan. Cook, stirring, for 2 minutes. Stir in the remaining stock and the soy sauce and rice wine, then add the pork, lemon grass, chilli and ginger. Season with salt and pepper. Bring to the boil, then lower the heat and simmer for 25 minutes.

Bring a separate saucepan of water to the boil, add the noodles and cook for 3 minutes. Remove from the heat, drain, then add the noodles to the soup along with the water chestnuts. Cook for a further 2 minutes, then remove from the heat and ladle into serving bowls.

SERVES 6-8

500 g/1 lb 2 oz split green peas
1 tbsp olive oil
1 large onion, finely chopped
1 large carrot, finely chopped

1 celery stick, finely chopped
1 litre/1¾ pints chicken or vegetable stock
1 litre/1¾ pints water
225 g/8 oz lean smoked ham, finely diced

¼ tsp dried thyme
¼ tsp dried marjoram
1 bay leaf
salt and pepper

Split Pea + Ham Soup

Rinse the peas under cold running water. Put in a saucepan and cover generously with water. Bring to the boil and boil for 3 minutes, skimming off the scum from the surface. Drain the peas.

Heat the oil in a large saucepan over a medium heat. Add the onion and cook for 3–4 minutes, stirring occasionally, until just softened.

Add the carrot and celery and continue cooking for 2 minutes. Add the peas, pour over the stock and water and stir to combine.

Bring just to the boil and stir the ham into the soup. Add the thyme, marjoram and bay leaf. Reduce the heat, cover and cook gently for 1–1½ hours, until the ingredients are very soft. Remove and discard the bay leaf.

Taste and adjust the seasoning, if necessary. Ladle into warmed soup bowls and serve.

SERVES 4

450 g/1 lb thick, rindless smoked bacon rashers, diced
1 onion, chopped
2 carrots, sliced

2 celery sticks, chopped
1 turnip, chopped
1 large potato, chopped
85 g/3 oz Puy lentils

1 bouquet garni
1 litre/1¾ pints chicken stock
salt and pepper

Bacon + Lentil Soup

Heat a large saucepan. Add the bacon and cook over a medium heat, stirring, for 4–5 minutes, or until the fat runs. Add the chopped onion, carrots, celery, turnip and potato and cook, stirring frequently, for 5 minutes.

Add the lentils and bouquet garni and pour in the stock. Bring to the boil, reduce the heat and simmer for 1 hour, or until the lentils are tender.

Remove and discard the bouquet garni and season the soup to taste with pepper, and with salt, if necessary. Ladle into warmed soup bowls and serve immediately.

SERVES 4

2 tbsp olive oil
2 garlic cloves, chopped
2 red onions, chopped
1 red pepper, deseeded and chopped
2 tbsp cornflour

1 litre/1¾ pints vegetable stock
450 g/1 lb potatoes, peeled, halved and sliced
150 g/5½ oz chorizo, sliced

2 courgettes, trimmed and sliced
200 g/7 oz canned red kidney beans, drained
125 ml/4 fl oz double cream
salt and pepper

Chorizo & Red Kidney Bean Soup

Heat the oil in a large saucepan. Add the garlic and onions and cook over a medium heat, stirring, for 3 minutes, until slightly softened. Add the red pepper and cook for a further 3 minutes, stirring. In a bowl, mix the cornflour with enough stock to make a smooth paste and stir it into the pan. Cook, stirring, for 2 minutes. Stir in the remaining stock, then add the potatoes and season to taste with salt and pepper. Bring to the boil, then lower the heat and simmer for 25 minutes, until the vegetables are tender.

Add the chorizo, courgettes and kidney beans to the pan. Cook for 10 minutes, then stir in the cream and cook for a further 5 minutes. Remove from the heat and ladle into serving bowls.

SERVES 4

3 tbsp butter
4 shallots, chopped
1 leek, sliced
450 g/1 lb skinless
  chicken breasts,
  chopped

600 ml/1 pint chicken
  stock
1 tbsp chopped fresh
  parsley
1 tbsp chopped fresh
  thyme, plus extra sprigs
  to garnish

175 ml/6 fl oz double
  cream
salt and pepper

Cream of Chicken Soup

Melt the butter in a large saucepan over a medium heat. Add the shallots and cook, stirring, for 3 minutes, until slightly softened. Add the leek and cook for a further 5 minutes, stirring. Add the chicken, stock and herbs, and season with salt and pepper. Bring to the boil, then lower the heat and simmer for 25 minutes, until the chicken is tender and cooked through. Remove from the heat and leave to cool for 10 minutes.

Transfer the soup to a food processor or blender and process until smooth (you may need to do this in batches). Return the soup to the rinsed-out pan and warm over a low heat for 5 minutes.

Stir in the cream and cook for a further 2 minutes, then remove from the heat and ladle into serving bowls. Garnish with sprigs of thyme and serve immediately.

SERVES 4–6

1–2 tbsp olive oil
2 onions, finely chopped
1–2 red chillies, deseeded and finely chopped
1 tsp ground cumin
1 tsp paprika
1 tsp granulated sugar

2 tsp dried mint
1 tbsp tomato purée
1.2 litres/2 pints chicken stock
100 g/3½ oz couscous
1 chicken, weighing 1.3 kg/3 lb, cooked and roughly torn into strips

salt and pepper
1 small bunch of fresh coriander, finely chopped, to garnish
1 lemon, quartered, to serve

Chicken Soup with Chilli, Mint & Couscous

Heat the oil in a heavy-based saucepan, add the onions and chillies and cook over a medium heat for 2–3 minutes, stirring frequently, until they begin to colour.

Add the cumin, paprika, sugar, mint and tomato purée and pour in the chicken stock. Bring to the boil and gradually stir in the couscous. Reduce the heat and simmer for 15 minutes. Stir in the strips of chicken, check the seasoning and adjust, if necessary, and simmer for a further 5 minutes.

Garnish the soup with the coriander and serve with the lemon quarters for squeezing over.

SERVES 4

4 tbsp butter
1 large onion, chopped
1 leek, trimmed and
  sliced
325 g/11½ oz cooked
  turkey meat, sliced

600 ml/1 pint chicken
  stock
150 g/5½ oz Stilton
  cheese, crumbled
150 ml/5 fl oz double
  cream

1 tbsp chopped fresh
  tarragon
pepper
fresh tarragon leaves and
  croûtons, to garnish

Turkey, Leek & Stilton Soup

Melt the butter in a saucepan over a medium heat. Add the onion and cook, stirring, for 4 minutes, until slightly softened. Add the leek and cook for another 3 minutes.

Add the turkey to the pan and pour in the stock. Bring to the boil, then reduce the heat and simmer gently, stirring occasionally, for about 15 minutes. Remove from the heat and leave to cool a little.

Transfer half of the soup into a food processor and blend until smooth. Return the mixture to the pan with the rest of the soup, stir in the Stilton, cream and tarragon and season to taste with pepper. Reheat gently, stirring. Remove from the heat, ladle into warmed soup bowls, garnish with tarragon and croûtons and serve.

SERVES 2

2 duck breasts, skin on
2 tbsp red curry paste
2 tbsp vegetable or
    groundnut oil
bunch of spring onions,
    chopped

2 garlic cloves, crushed
5-cm/2-inch piece fresh
    ginger, grated
2 carrots, thinly sliced
1 red pepper, deseeded
    and cut into strips

1 litre/1¾ pints chicken
    stock
2 tbsp sweet chilli sauce
3–4 tbsp Thai soy sauce
400 g/14 oz canned
    straw mushrooms,
    drained

Duck with Spring Onion Soup

Slash the skin of the duck 3–4 times with a sharp knife and rub in the curry paste. Cook the duck breasts, skin-side down, in a wok or frying pan over a high heat for 2–3 minutes. Turn over, reduce the heat and cook for a further 3–4 minutes, until cooked through. Lift out and slice thickly. Set aside and keep warm.

Meanwhile, heat the oil in a wok or large frying pan and stir-fry half the spring onions, the garlic, ginger, carrots and red pepper for 2–3 minutes. Pour in the stock and add the chilli sauce, soy sauce and mushrooms. Bring to the boil, lower the heat and simmer for 4–5 minutes.

Ladle the soup into warmed bowls, top with the duck slices and garnish with the remaining spring onions. Serve immediately.

SERVES 4

1 litre/1¾ pints water
2 tsp dashi granules
175 g/6 oz silken tofu,
   drained and cut into
   small cubes

4 shiitake mushrooms,
   finely sliced
4 tbsp miso paste
2 spring onions, chopped

Miso Soup

Put the water in a large pan with the dashi granules and bring to the boil. Add the tofu and mushrooms, reduce the heat, and let simmer for 3 minutes.

Stir in the miso paste and let simmer gently, stirring, until it has dissolved.

Add the spring onions and serve immediately. If you leave the soup, the miso will settle, so give the soup a thorough stir before serving to recombine.

SERVES 4

2 tbsp olive oil
3 rashers rindless, smoked bacon, finely chopped
25 g/1 oz butter
450 g/1 lb floury potatoes, chopped

450 g/1 lb onions, finely chopped
600 ml/1 pint chicken stock
600 ml/1 pint milk
100 g/3½ oz dried conchigliette

150 ml/5 fl oz double cream
2 tbsp chopped parsley
2 tbsp pesto
salt and pepper
Parmesan cheese shavings, to serve

Potato & Pesto Soup

Heat the oil in a large saucepan and cook the bacon over a medium heat for 4 minutes. Add the butter, potatoes and onions and cook for 12 minutes, stirring constantly.

Add the stock and milk to the saucepan, bring to the boil and simmer for 5 minutes. Add the conchigliette and simmer for a further 3–4 minutes.

Blend in the cream and simmer for 5 minutes. Add the parsley, salt and pepper to taste and pesto. Ladle the soup into warmed bowls, top with Parmesan cheese shavings and serve.

SERVES 6

25 g/1 oz butter
1 onion, chopped
1 garlic clove, finely
   chopped
55 g/2 oz rindless streaky
   bacon, diced
2 celery sticks, chopped

400 g/14 oz canned
   chopped tomatoes
150 ml/5 fl oz dry white
   wine
300 ml/10 fl oz fish stock
4 fresh basil leaves, torn
2 tbsp chopped fresh
   flat-leaf parsley

450 g/1 lb white fish
   fillets, such as cod or
   monkfish, skinned and
   chopped
115 g/4 oz cooked
   peeled prawns
salt and pepper

Genoese Fish Soup

Melt the butter in a large, heavy-based saucepan. Add the onion and garlic and cook over a low heat, stirring occasionally, for 5 minutes, or until softened.

Add the streaky bacon and celery and cook, stirring frequently, for a further 2 minutes.

Add the tomatoes, wine, stock, basil and 1 tablespoon of the parsley. Season to taste with salt and pepper. Bring to the boil, then reduce the heat and simmer for 10 minutes.

Add the fish and cook for 5 minutes, or until it is opaque. Add the prawns and heat through gently for 3 minutes. Ladle into warmed serving bowls, garnish with the remaining chopped parsley and serve immediately.

SERVES 4

4 tbsp olive oil
3 leeks, sliced
2 celery sticks, chopped
1 large onion, chopped
2 large garlic cloves, crushed
250 g/9 oz chestnut mushrooms, sliced
1 litre/1¾ pints fish stock

250 g/9 oz canned tomatoes
100 ml/3½ fl oz Italian dry white wine
1 tsp hot paprika
450 g/1 lb mixed fish fillets, such as cod, sea bass, monkfish, cut into bite-sized pieces

450 g/1 lb mixed raw seafood, such as prawns, peeled and deveined, mussels in their shells, squid, cut into rings and tentacles chopped, and cooked crabmeat
salt and pepper
chopped fresh flat-leaf parsley, to garnish

Italian Fish Soup with White Wine

Heat the oil in a large saucepan over a medium heat, add the leeks, celery, onion and garlic and cook, stirring frequently, for 8–10 minutes, or until softened. Add the mushrooms, stock, tomatoes and their juice and wine and stir well.

Bring to a simmer and add the paprika and season to taste with salt and pepper. Then add all the fish and seafood and simmer gently for 15 minutes. Taste and adjust the seasoning, if necessary. Discard any mussels that haven't opened.

Ladle into warmed bowls, garnish with parsley and serve.

SERVES 4

1 tbsp olive oil
1 large onion, finely
  chopped
3 large leeks, including
  green parts, thinly
  sliced

1 potato, finely diced
450 ml/16 fl oz fish stock
700 ml/1¼ pints water
1 bay leaf
300 g/10½ oz skinless
  salmon fillet, cut into
  1-cm/½-inch cubes

80 ml/3 fl oz double
  cream
fresh lemon juice
  (optional)
salt and pepper
sprigs of fresh chervil or
  parsley, to garnish

Salmon + Leek Soup

Heat the oil in a heavy-based saucepan over a medium heat. Add the onion and leeks and cook for about 3 minutes until they begin to soften.

Add the potato, stock, water and bay leaf with a large pinch of salt. Bring to the boil, reduce the heat, cover and cook gently for about 25 minutes, or until the vegetables are tender. Remove and discard the bay leaf.

Allow the soup to cool slightly, then transfer about half of it to a food processor or blender and process until smooth. (If using a food processor, strain off the cooking liquid and reserve. Purée half the soup solids with enough cooking liquid to moisten them, then combine with the remaining liquid.)

Return the puréed soup to the saucepan and stir to blend. Reheat gently over a medium–low heat.

Season the salmon with salt and pepper and add to the soup. Continue cooking for about 5 minutes, stirring occasionally, until the fish is tender and starts to break up. Stir in the cream, taste and adjust the seasoning, adding a little lemon juice, if using. Ladle into warmed bowls, garnish with chervil or parsley and serve.

SERVES 4

4 tsp butter
1 large onion, finely chopped
1 small carrot, finely diced
3 tbsp plain flour

300 ml/10 fl oz fish stock
200 ml/7 fl oz water
450 g/1 lb potatoes, diced
125 g/4½ oz cooked or defrosted frozen sweetcorn

450 ml/16 fl oz milk
280 g/10 oz canned clams, drained and rinsed
salt and pepper
chopped fresh parsley, to garnish

Clam & Corn Chowder

Melt the butter in a large saucepan over a medium–low heat. Add the onion and carrot and cook for 3–4 minutes, stirring frequently, until the onion is softened. Stir in the flour and continue cooking for 2 minutes.

Slowly add about half the stock and stir well, scraping the bottom of the pan to mix in the flour. Pour in the remaining stock and the water and bring just to the boil, stirring.

Add the potatoes, sweetcorn and milk and stir to combine. Reduce the heat and simmer gently, partially covered, for about 20 minutes, stirring occasionally, until all the vegetables are tender.

Chop the clams, if large. Stir in the clams and continue cooking for about 5 minutes until heated through. Taste and adjust the seasoning, if necessary.

Ladle the soup into warmed bowls, sprinkle with the parsley and serve.

SERVES 4

20–24 large raw
  unpeeled prawns
450 ml/16 fl oz fish stock
pinch of salt
1 tsp groundnut oil
450 ml/16 fl oz coconut
  milk
2 tsp nam pla
  (Thai fish sauce)
½ tbsp lime juice

115 g/4 oz dried medium
  rice noodles
55 g/2 oz beansprouts
sprigs of fresh coriander,
  to garnish

laksa paste
6 coriander stalks with
  leaves
3 large garlic cloves,
  crushed

1 fresh red chilli,
  deseeded and
  chopped
1 lemon grass stalk,
  centre part only,
  chopped
2.5-cm/1-inch piece fresh
  ginger, peeled and
  chopped
1½ tbsp shrimp paste
½ tsp turmeric
2 tbsp groundnut oil

Prawn Laksa

Peel and devein the prawns. Put the fish stock, salt and the prawn heads, peels and tails in a saucepan over a high heat and bring to the boil. Lower the heat and simmer for 10 minutes.

Meanwhile, make the laksa paste. Put all the ingredients except the oil in a food processor and blend. With the motor running, slowly add up to 2 tablespoons of oil just until a paste forms. (If your food processor is too large to work efficiently with this small quantity, use a pestle and mortar, or make double the quantity and keep the leftovers tightly covered in the refrigerator to use another time.)

Heat the 1 teaspoon of groundnut oil in a large saucepan over a high heat. Add the paste and stir-fry until it is fragrant. Strain the stock through a sieve lined with muslin. Stir the stock into the laksa paste, along with the coconut milk, nam pla and lime juice. Bring to the boil, then lower the heat, cover and simmer for 30 minutes.

Meanwhile, soak the noodles in a large bowl with enough lukewarm water to cover for 20 minutes, until soft. Alternatively, cook according to the packet instructions. Drain and set aside.

Add the prawns and beansprouts to the stew and continue simmering just until the prawns turn opaque and curl. Divide the noodles among 4 warmed bowls and ladle the soup over the top. Garnish with coriander and serve.

SERVES 6

1 kg/2 lb 4 oz live mussels
4 tbsp plain flour
1.5 litres/2¾ pints fish
   stock
1 tbsp butter

1 large onion, finely
   chopped
350 g/12 oz skinless white
   fish fillets, such as cod,
   sole or haddock
200 g/7 oz raw prawns,
   peeled and deveined

300 ml/10 fl oz whipping
   cream or double
   cream
salt and pepper
snipped fresh dill,
   to garnish

Seafood Chowder

Discard any mussels with broken shells or any that refuse to close when tapped. Rinse and pull off any beards. Put the mussels in a large, heavy-based saucepan. Cover tightly and cook over a high heat for about 4 minutes, or until the mussels open, shaking the pan occasionally. Discard any that remain closed. When they are cool enough to handle, remove the mussels from their shells and set aside.

Put the flour in a mixing bowl and very slowly whisk in enough of the stock to make a thick paste. Whisk in a little more stock to make a smooth liquid.

Melt the butter in a heavy-based saucepan over a medium–low heat. Add the onion, cover and cook for 3 minutes, stirring frequently, until it softens.

Add the remaining fish stock and bring to the boil. Slowly whisk in the flour mixture until well combined and bring back to the boil, whisking constantly. Add the mussel cooking liquid. Season with salt, if needed, and pepper. Reduce the heat and simmer, partially covered, for 15 minutes.

Add the fish and mussels and continue simmering, stirring occasionally, for about 5 minutes, or until the fish is cooked and begins to flake.

Stir in the prawns and cream. Taste and adjust the seasoning, if necessary. Simmer for a few minutes longer to heat through. Ladle into warmed bowls, sprinkle with dill and serve.

SERVES 2

300 g/10½ oz raw prawns, peeled and deveined
2 tsp vegetable oil
2 fresh red chillies, sliced
1 garlic clove, sliced
about 750 ml/1⅓ pints fish stock

4 thin slices fresh ginger
2 lemon grass stalks, bruised
5 Thai lime leaves, shredded
2 tsp palm sugar or brown sugar

1 tbsp chilli oil
handful of fresh coriander leaves
dash of lime juice

Hot & Sour Prawn Soup

Dry fry the prawns in a frying pan or wok until they turn pink. Remove and set aside.

Heat the vegetable oil in the same pan, add the chillies and garlic and cook for 30 seconds.

Add the stock, ginger, lemon grass, Thai lime leaves and sugar and simmer for 4 minutes. Add the reserved prawns with the chilli oil and coriander and cook for 1–2 minutes.

Stir in the lime juice and serve immediately.

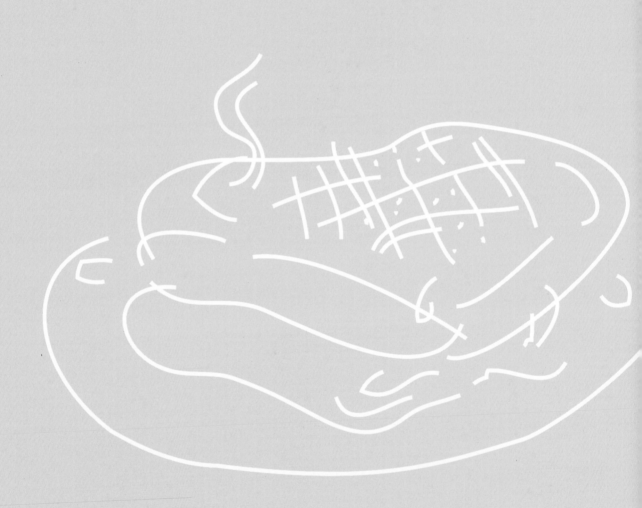

Meat & Poultry

SERVES 4–6

1.3 kg/3 lb stewing steak, cubed
2 tbsp vegetable oil
4 onions, finely chopped
4 tbsp sweet paprika
2 tbsp tomato purée

1 tsp caraway or dill seeds
2 tsp wine vinegar
4 green peppers, deseeded and diced
1 large garlic clove, finely chopped

5 medium potatoes, peeled and cubed
350–450 ml/12–16 fl oz hot meat stock
3 tbsp chopped fresh dill
salt and pepper
soured cream, to serve

Hungarian Beef Goulash

Put the meat in a shallow dish and sprinkle with 1 teaspoon of salt. Toss to mix, then cover and leave to stand for 15 minutes. Preheat the oven to 160°C/325°F/ Gas Mark 3.

Heat a heavy-based casserole over a medium heat. Add the oil and gently fry the onions until soft but not coloured. Season with another teaspoon of salt, then stir in the paprika and tomato purée, and cook for a minute or two. Stir in the caraway seeds, vinegar and ½ teaspoon of pepper. Add the green peppers and garlic, and cook for a few more minutes.

Add the meat to the casserole, stirring well to coat. Cover tightly and cook in the oven for 1 hour, stirring every 30 minutes to submerge the meat in the juices (which should come slightly below the top of the meat). Add the potatoes, and cook for another hour, stirring halfway through, until the meat is tender.

Pour in enough hot stock to come just above the meat. Cover and cook for another 22–30 minutes. Taste and adjust the seasoning, if necessary. Sprinkle with the chopped dill and serve with soured cream.

SERVES 6

2 tbsp sunflower oil
2 large onions, thinly
  sliced
8 carrots, sliced
4 tbsp plain flour
1.25 kg/2 lb 12 oz stewing
  steak, cut into cubes

425 ml/15 fl oz stout
2 tsp muscovado sugar
2 bay leaves
1 tbsp chopped fresh
  thyme
salt and pepper

herb dumplings
115 g/4 oz self-raising
  flour
pinch of salt
55 g/2 oz shredded suet
2 tbsp chopped fresh
  parsley, plus extra
  to garnish
about 4 tbsp water

Beef in Beer with Herb Dumplings

Preheat the oven to 160°C/325°F/Gas Mark 3. Heat the oil in a flameproof casserole. Add the onions and carrots and cook over a low heat, stirring occasionally, for 5 minutes, or until the onions are softened. Meanwhile, place the flour in a polythene bag and season with salt and pepper. Add the stewing steak to the bag, tie the top and shake well to coat. Do this in batches, if necessary.

Remove the vegetables from the casserole with a slotted spoon and reserve. Add the stewing steak to the casserole, in batches, and cook, stirring frequently, until browned all over. Return all the meat and the onions and carrots to the casserole and sprinkle in any remaining seasoned flour. Pour in the stout and add the sugar, bay leaves and thyme. Bring to the boil, cover and transfer to the preheated oven to bake for 1¾ hours.

To make the herb dumplings, sift the flour and salt into a bowl. Stir in the suet and parsley and add enough of the water to make a soft dough. Shape into small balls between the palms of your hands. Add to the casserole and return to the oven for 30 minutes. Remove and discard the bay leaves. Serve immediately, sprinkled with chopped parsley.

SERVES 4

450 g/1 lb stewing steak
1½ tbsp plain flour
1 tsp hot paprika
1–1½ tsp chilli powder
1 tsp ground ginger
2 tbsp olive oil
1 large onion, cut into
chunks
3 garlic cloves, sliced

2 celery sticks, sliced
225 g/8 oz carrots,
chopped
300 ml/10 fl oz lager
300 ml/10 fl oz beef stock
350 g/12 oz potatoes,
chopped
1 red pepper, deseeded
and chopped

2 corn on the cob,
halved
115 g/4 oz tomatoes,
quartered
115 g/4 oz shelled fresh
or frozen peas
1 tbsp chopped fresh
coriander
salt and pepper

Beef & Vegetable Stew

Trim any fat or gristle from the beef and cut into 2.5-cm/1-inch chunks. Mix the flour and spices together. Toss the beef in the spiced flour until well coated.

Heat the oil in a large, heavy-based saucepan and cook the onion, garlic and celery, stirring frequently, for 5 minutes, or until softened. Add the beef and cook over a high heat, stirring frequently, for 3 minutes, or until browned on all sides and sealed.

Add the carrots, then remove from the heat. Gradually stir in the lager and stock, then return to the heat and bring to the boil, stirring. Reduce the heat, cover and simmer, stirring occasionally, for 1½ hours.

Add the potatoes to the saucepan and simmer for a further 15 minutes. Add the red pepper and corn on the cob and simmer for a further 15 minutes, then add the tomatoes and peas and simmer for a further 10 minutes, or until the beef and vegetables are tender. Season to taste with salt and pepper, stir in the coriander and serve.

SERVES 4

400 g/14 oz lean beef
2 low-salt lean smoked back bacon rashers
12 shallots, peeled
1 garlic clove, crushed

225 g/8 oz closed-cup mushrooms, sliced
300 ml/10 fl oz red wine
425 ml/15 fl oz beef stock
2 bay leaves
2 tbsp chopped fresh thyme

55 g/2 oz cornflour
100 ml/3½ fl oz cold water
pepper
boiled rice and seasonal vegetables, to serve

Boeuf Bourguignon

Trim any visible fat from the beef and bacon and cut the meat into bite-sized pieces. Put the meat into a large saucepan with the shallots, garlic, mushrooms, wine, stock, bay leaves and 1 tablespoon of the thyme. Bring to the boil, then reduce the heat, cover and simmer for 50 minutes, or until the meat and shallots are tender.

Blend the cornflour with the water in a small bowl and stir into the casserole. Return to the boil, stirring constantly, and cook until the casserole thickens. Reduce the heat and simmer for a further 5 minutes. Season to taste with pepper.

Remove and discard the bay leaves. Transfer the boeuf bourguignon to a warmed casserole dish and sprinkle over the remaining thyme. Serve with boiled rice and seasonal vegetables.

SERVES 4

350 g/12 oz fresh lean
beef mince
1 large onion, finely
chopped
1 tsp dried mixed herbs
1 tbsp plain flour
300 ml/10 fl oz beef stock

1 tbsp tomato purée
2 large tomatoes, thinly
sliced
4 courgettes, thinly sliced
2 tbsp cornflour
300 ml/10 fl oz skimmed
milk

150 ml/5 fl oz low-fat
natural fromage frais
1 egg yolk
4 tbsp freshly grated
Parmesan cheese
salt and pepper

Beef + Tomato Gratin

Preheat the oven to 190°C/375°F/Gas Mark 5. In a large frying pan, dry-fry the beef and onion for 4–5 minutes, or until browned.

Stir in the herbs, flour, stock and tomato purée, and season to taste with salt and pepper. Bring to the boil, then reduce the heat and simmer for 30 minutes, or until thickened.

Transfer the beef mixture to an ovenproof gratin dish. Cover with a layer of the sliced tomatoes and then add a layer of sliced courgettes. Set aside until required.

Blend the cornflour with a little of the milk in a small bowl. Pour the remaining milk into a saucepan and bring to the boil. Add the cornflour mixture and cook, stirring, for 1–2 minutes, or until thickened. Remove from the heat and beat in the fromage frais and egg yolk. Season well.

Spread the white sauce over the layer of courgettes. Place the dish on a baking sheet and sprinkle with Parmesan cheese. Bake in the oven for 25–30 minutes, or until golden brown. Serve immediately.

SERVES 6

2½ tbsp plain flour
1 tsp salt
¼ tsp pepper
1 rolled brisket joint, weighing 1.6 kg/ 3 lb 8 oz
2 tbsp vegetable oil

2 tbsp butter
1 onion, finely chopped
2 celery sticks, diced
2 carrots, peeled and diced
1 tsp dill seed
1 tsp dried thyme or oregano

350 ml/12 fl oz red wine
150–225 ml/5–8 fl oz beef stock
4–5 potatoes, cut into large chunks and boiled until just tender
2 tbsp chopped fresh dill, to serve

Pot Roast with Potatoes & Dill

Preheat the oven to 140°C/275°F/Gas Mark 1. Mix 2 tablespoons of the flour with the salt and pepper in a shallow dish. Dip the meat to coat. Heat the oil in a flameproof casserole and brown the meat all over. Transfer to a plate. Add half the butter to the casserole and cook the onion, celery, carrots, dill seed and thyme for 5 minutes. Return the meat and juices to the casserole.

Pour in the wine and enough stock to reach one third of the way up the meat. Bring to the boil, cover and cook in the oven for 3 hours, turning the meat every 30 minutes. After it has been cooking for 2 hours, add the potatoes and more stock if necessary.

When ready, transfer the meat and vegetables to a warmed serving dish. Strain the cooking liquid to remove any solids, then return the liquid to the casserole.

Mix the remaining butter and flour to a paste. Bring the cooking liquid to the boil. Whisk in small pieces of the flour and butter paste, whisking constantly until the sauce is smooth. Pour the sauce over the meat and vegetables. Sprinkle with the fresh dill to serve.

SERVES 4

2 beef tomatoes, cut into thick slices
2 red onions, each cut into 6 wedges
4 large garlic cloves, peeled
1 tsp sea salt

3 tbsp olive oil, plus extra for brushing
1 heaped tsp dried Herbes de Provence
4 lamb steaks, about 175 g/6 oz each
pepper

to serve
4 wholemeal pitta breads
50 g/1¾ oz pine kernels, toasted
1 handful fresh basil leaves
200 ml/7 fl oz thick natural yogurt

Tray-Baked Lamb Steaks with Tomatoes

Preheat the oven to 190°C/375°F/Gas Mark 5. Arrange the tomato slices and onion wedges in a roasting tin. Put the garlic cloves and salt in a mortar and crush to a purée with a pestle. Work in the oil. Spoon the mixture over the vegetables and mix well. Sprinkle over the herbs and season to taste with pepper. Put on the top shelf of the preheated oven and roast for 20 minutes.

Meanwhile, lightly brush the lamb steaks with oil. Heat a non-stick frying pan over a high heat. When very hot, add the lamb steaks and cook for 1 minute on each side to sear.

Remove the roasting tin from the oven. Turn the vegetables over, arrange the lamb steaks on top and spoon over the juices from the corners of the tin, adding a little water if too dry. Return the tin to the oven and roast for a further 15–20 minutes until the vegetables are tender and the lamb is cooked to your liking. Sprinkle the pitta breads with water and put them in the oven for the last 1–2 minutes of the cooking time.

Scatter the pine kernels and basil over the lamb and vegetables before serving, adding a portion of yogurt and a warmed pitta bread to each plate.

SERVES 4

2 tbsp olive oil
4 lamb shanks, about
    300 g/10½ oz each
2 onions, sliced
2 peppers, any colour,
    deseeded and
    chopped
2 garlic cloves, well
    crushed

1 aubergine, cut into
    small cubes
½ tsp paprika
½ tsp ground cinnamon
200 g/7 oz cooked
    chickpeas
400 g/14 oz canned
    chopped tomatoes

2 tsp mixed dried
    Mediterranean herbs
100 ml/3½ fl oz lamb or
    vegetable stock, plus
    extra if needed salt and
    pepper
Couscous, to serve

Turkish Lamb Casserole

Preheat the oven to 160°C/325°F/Gas Mark 3. Heat half the oil in a large, non-stick frying pan over a high heat, add the lamb shanks and cook, turning frequently, for 2–3 minutes until browned all over. Transfer to a casserole.

Heat the remaining oil in the frying pan over a medium–high heat, add the onions and peppers and cook, stirring frequently, for 10–15 minutes, or until the onions are thoroughly soft and just turning golden. Add the garlic, aubergine and spices and cook, stirring constantly, for 1 minute. Add the chickpeas, tomatoes and their juice, herbs and enough stock to cover the base of the frying pan by about 2 cm/¾ inch, stir well and bring to a simmer. Season to taste with salt and pepper and transfer to a casserole.

Cover the casserole, transfer to the middle shelf of the preheated oven and cook for 1 hour. Check after 45 minutes that the casserole is gently bubbling and that there is enough liquid – if it looks rather dry, add a little more stock or boiling water and stir in. If bubbling too much, reduce the oven temperature. Serve with freshly cooked couscous.

SERVES 4

4 lamb leg steaks
4 tsp ground coriander
1 tbsp ground cumin
1 small butternut squash
1 tbsp olive oil
1 onion, chopped

600 ml/1 pint chicken
  stock
2 tbsp chopped fresh
  ginger
100 g/3½ oz ready-to-eat
  dried apricots
2 tbsp clear honey

finely grated rind and
  juice of 1 lemon
200 g/7 oz couscous
salt and pepper
3 tbsp chopped fresh
  mint, to garnish

Honeyed Apricot Lamb with Lemon Couscous

Sprinkle the lamb steaks with the ground coriander and cumin then peel and deseed the squash and cut into bite-sized chunks.

Heat the oil in a flameproof casserole. Add the lamb and cook over a high heat for 2–3 minutes, turning once. Stir in the squash, onion and half the stock, then bring to the boil.

Add the ginger, apricots, honey and lemon juice and season to taste with salt and pepper. Cover and cook over a medium heat for about 20 minutes, stirring occasionally.

Meanwhile, bring the remaining stock to the boil in a small saucepan, then stir in the couscous and lemon rind and season to taste with salt and pepper. Remove from the heat, cover and leave to stand for 5 minutes. Serve the lamb with the couscous, sprinkled with fresh mint.

SERVES 4-6

6 tbsp olive oil
225 g/8 oz chorizo
  sausage, cut into
  5-mm/¼-inch thick
  slices, casings removed
2 large onions, chopped
6 large garlic cloves,
  crushed
900 g/2 lb boned leg of
  lamb, cut into 5-cm/
  2-inch cubes

250 ml/9 fl oz lamb stock
  or water
125 ml/4 fl oz red wine,
  such as Rioja or
  Tempranillo
2 tbsp sherry vinegar
800 g/1 lb 12 oz canned
  chopped tomatoes
4 sprigs fresh thyme, plus
  extra to garnish
2 bay leaves

½ tsp sweet Spanish
  paprika
800 g/1 lb 12 oz canned
  chickpeas, rinsed and
  drained
salt and pepper

Lamb Stew with Chickpeas

Preheat the oven to 160°C/325°F/Gas Mark 3. Heat 4 tablespoons of the oil in a large, heavy-based flameproof casserole over a medium–high heat. Reduce the heat, add the chorizo and fry for 1 minute and then set aside. Add the onions to the casserole and fry for 2 minutes, then add the garlic and continue frying for 3 minutes, or until the onions are soft, but not brown. Remove from the casserole and set aside.

Heat the remaining 2 tablespoons of oil in the casserole. Add the lamb cubes in a single layer without over-crowding the casserole, and fry until browned on each side; work in batches, if necessary.

Return the onion mixture to the casserole with all the lamb. Stir in the stock, wine, vinegar, tomatoes with their juices and season to taste with salt and pepper. Bring to the boil, scraping any glazed bits from the base of the casserole. Reduce the heat and stir in the thyme, bay leaves and paprika.

Transfer to the preheated oven and cook, covered, for 40–45 minutes, or until the lamb is tender. Stir in the chickpeas and return to the oven, uncovered, for 10 minutes, or until they are heated through and the juices are reduced.

Taste and adjust the seasoning, if necessary. Serve garnished with thyme.

SERVES 4

450 g/1 lb lean boneless lamb, such as leg of lamb or fillet
1½ tbsp plain flour
1 tsp ground cloves
1–1½ tbsp olive oil
1 white onion, sliced

2–3 garlic cloves, sliced
300 ml/10 fl oz orange juice
150 ml/5 fl oz lamb stock or chicken stock
1 cinnamon stick, bruised
2 red peppers, deseeded and sliced into rings

4 tomatoes
few fresh sprigs coriander, plus 1 tbsp chopped fresh coriander, to garnish
salt and pepper

Lamb Stew with Sweet Red Peppers

Preheat the oven to 190°C/375°F/Gas Mark 5. Trim any fat or gristle from the lamb and cut into thin strips. Mix the flour and cloves together. Toss the lamb in the spiced flour until well coated and reserve any remaining spiced flour.

Heat 1 tablespoon of the oil in a heavy-based frying pan and cook the lamb over a high heat, stirring frequently, for 3 minutes, or until browned on all sides and sealed. Using a slotted spoon, transfer to an ovenproof casserole.

Add the onion and garlic to the frying pan and cook over a medium heat, stirring frequently, for 3 minutes, adding the extra oil if necessary. Sprinkle in the reserved spiced flour and cook, stirring constantly, for 2 minutes, then remove from the heat.

Gradually stir in the orange juice and stock, then return to the heat and bring to the boil, stirring.

Pour over the lamb in the casserole, add the cinnamon stick, red peppers, tomatoes and coriander sprigs and stir well. Cover and cook in the preheated oven for 1½ hours, or until the lamb is tender.

Discard the cinnamon stick and taste and adjust the seasoning, if necessary. Serve garnished with the chopped coriander.

SERVES 4

225 g/8 oz black-eyed beans, soaked overnight in cold water and drained
3 tbsp sunflower oil
1 kg/2 lb 4 oz boneless leg of lamb, cut into cubes

4 leeks, sliced
1 parsnip, cut into cubes
3 carrots, thickly sliced
2 small turnips, cut into cubes
150 ml/5 fl oz beef stock

2 tbsp chopped fresh parsley
1 small fresh rosemary sprig
1 tbsp mint or redcurrant jelly
salt and pepper

Lamb + Bean Stew

Put the beans into a saucepan, add cold water to cover and bring to the boil. Boil for 15 minutes, drain and set aside.

Heat the oil in a large frying pan. Add the meat and cook over a medium heat, stirring frequently, for about 8 minutes, until browned. Remove with a slotted spoon and set aside. Add the leeks, parsnip, carrots and turnips to the pan and cook, stirring frequently, for about 8 minutes, until beginning to colour. Remove with a slotted spoon and set aside. Pour the stock into the pan, add the herbs and mint jelly and bring to the boil, scraping up the sediment from the base. Remove from the heat.

Bring a saucepan of water to the boil. Mix together the lamb, vegetables and beans, season to taste with salt and pepper and spoon into a 1.2-litre/2-pint heatproof pudding basin. Pour in the stock mixture. Cut a circle of foil 5 cm/2 inches larger than the circumference of the top of the basin, make a pleat in the centre and put it over the basin. Tie in place with string. Put the basin into a steamer, cover with a tight-fitting lid and set it over the pan. Steam for 1¾ hours.

Transfer the lamb, vegetables and beans to a serving dish. Remove and discard the rosemary sprig. Pour the liquid into a saucepan and boil until reduced. Pour over the stew and serve immediately.

SERVES 4

plain flour, for coating
450 g/1 lb boneless pork,
  cut into 2.5-cm/1-inch
  cubes
1 tbsp vegetable oil
225 g/8 oz chorizo
  sausage, outer casing
  removed, cut into
  bite-sized chunks
1 onion, roughly
  chopped

4 garlic cloves, finely
  chopped
2 celery stalks, chopped
1 cinnamon stick, broken
2 bay leaves
2 tsp allspice
2 carrots, sliced
2–3 fresh red chillies,
  deseeded and finely
  chopped

6 ripe tomatoes, peeled
  and chopped
1 litre/1¾ pints pork or
  vegetable stock
2 sweet potatoes, cut into
  chunks
corn kernels, cut from
  1 ear fresh sweetcorn
1 tbsp chopped fresh
  oregano
salt and pepper
fresh oregano, to garnish

Spicy Pork + Vegetable Hotpot

Season the flour well with salt and pepper and toss the pork in it to coat. Heat the oil in a large, heavy-based saucepan or ovenproof casserole. Add the chorizo and lightly brown on all sides. Remove the chorizo with a slotted spoon and set aside.

Add the pork, in batches, and cook until browned on all sides. Remove the pork with a slotted spoon and set aside. Add the onion, garlic and celery to the pan and cook for 5 minutes, or until softened.

Add the cinnamon, bay leaves and allspice and cook, stirring, for 2 minutes. Add the pork, carrots, chillies, tomatoes and stock. Bring to the boil, then reduce the heat, cover and simmer for 1 hour, or until the pork is tender.

Return the chorizo to the pan with the sweet potatoes, corn, oregano and season to taste with salt and pepper. Cover and simmer for a further 30 minutes, or until the vegetables are tender. Serve garnished with oregano.

SERVES 4

2 tbsp olive oil
1 onion, sliced
1 large yellow pepper,
   deseeded and sliced
1 garlic clove, crushed
1 tsp chilli flakes

225 g/8 oz chorizo
   sausage
400 g/14 oz canned
   chopped tomatoes
400 g/14 oz canned
   chickpeas, drained

200 g/7 oz basmati rice
handful of rocket leaves
salt and pepper
4 tbsp roughly chopped
   fresh basil, to garnish

Chorizo, Chilli & Chickpea Casserole

Heat the oil in a flameproof casserole and fry the onion over a medium heat, stirring occasionally, for 5 minutes. Add the yellow pepper, garlic and chilli flakes and cook for 2 minutes, stirring.

Chop the chorizo into bite-sized chunks and stir into the casserole. Add the tomatoes and chickpeas and season to taste with salt and pepper. Bring to the boil, cover and simmer for 10 minutes.

Meanwhile, cook the rice in a saucepan of lightly salted boiling water for 10–12 minutes, until tender. Drain and stir the rocket into the casserole. Serve spooned over the rice, garnished with fresh basil.

SERVES 4

450–550 g/1–1 lb 4 oz lean gammon
2½ tbsp olive oil, plus 1–2 tsp
1 onion, chopped
2–3 garlic cloves, chopped
2 celery sticks, chopped

175 g/6 oz sliced carrots
1 cinnamon stick, bruised
½ tsp ground cloves
¼ tsp freshly grated nutmeg
1 tsp dried oregano
450 ml/16 fl oz chicken stock or vegetable stock
1–2 tbsp maple syrup

3 large spicy sausages, or about 225 g/8 oz chorizo
400 g/14 oz canned black-eyed beans or broad beans
1 orange pepper
1 tbsp cornflour
pepper

Ham with Black-Eyed Beans

Trim off any fat or skin from the ham and cut into 4-cm/1½-inch chunks. Heat 1 tablespoon of the oil in a heavy-based pan and cook the ham over high heat, stirring frequently, for 5 minutes, or until browned on all sides and sealed. Using a slotted spoon, remove from the pan and set aside.

Add the onion, garlic, celery and carrots to the pan with an additional 1 tablespoon of the oil if necessary and cook over a medium heat, stirring frequently, for 5 minutes, or until softened. Add all the spices and season to taste with salt and pepper, then cook, stirring constantly, for 2 minutes.

Return the ham to the pan. Add the dried oregano, stock and maple syrup to taste, then bring to the boil, stirring. Reduce the heat, then cover and simmer, stirring occasionally, for 1 hour.

Heat the remaining 1–2 tablespoons of the oil in a frying pan and cook the sausages, turning frequently, until browned all over. Remove and cut each into 3–4 chunks, then add to the pan. Drain and rinse the beans, then drain again. Deseed and chop the orange pepper.

Add the beans and pepper to the pan, and simmer for an additional 20 minutes. Blend 2 tablespoons of water with the cornflour and stir into the stew, then cook for 3–5 minutes. Remove and discard the cinnamon stick before serving.

SERVES 4

450 g/1 lb lean boneless pork
1½ tbsp plain flour
1 tsp ground coriander
1 tsp ground cumin
1½ tsp ground cinnamon
1 tbsp olive oil
1 onion, chopped

400 g/14 oz canned chopped tomatoes
2 tbsp tomato purée
450 ml/16 fl oz chicken stock
225 g/8 oz carrots, chopped
350 g/12 oz squash, such as kabocha, peeled, seeded, and chopped

225 g/8 oz leeks, sliced, blanched, and drained
115 g/4 oz/ okra, trimmed and sliced
salt and pepper
sprigs of fresh parsley, to garnish
couscous, to serve

Pork & Vegetable Stew

Trim off any fat or gristle from the pork and cut into thin strips about 5 cm/2 inches long. Mix the flour and spices together. Toss the pork in the spiced flour until well coated and reserve any remaining spiced flour.

Heat the oil in a large, heavy-based pan and cook the onion, stirring frequently, for 5 minutes, or until softened. Add the pork and cook over a high heat, stirring frequently, for 5 minutes, or until browned on all sides and sealed. Sprinkle in the reserved spiced flour and cook, stirring constantly, for 2 minutes, then remove from the heat.

Gradually add the tomatoes to the pan. Blend the tomato purée with a little of the stock in a jug and gradually stir into the pan, then stir in half the remaining stock.

Add the carrots, then return to the heat and bring to a boil, stirring. Reduce the heat, then cover and simmer, stirring occasionally, for 1½ hours. Add the squash and cook for an additional 15 minutes.

Add the leeks and okra, and the remaining stock if you prefer a thinner stew. Simmer for an additional 15 minutes, or until the pork and vegetables are tender. Season to taste with salt and pepper, then garnish with fresh parsley and serve with couscous.

SERVES 4

350 g/12 oz lean pork
    fillet
1 tbsp vegetable oil
1 medium onion,
    chopped
2 garlic cloves, crushed
25 g/1 oz plain flour
2 tbsp tomato purée

425 ml/15 fl oz chicken or
    vegetable stock
125 g/4½ oz button
    mushrooms, sliced
1 large green pepper,
    deseeded and
    chopped
½ tsp freshly grated
    nutmeg, plus extra
    to garnish

4 tbsp low-fat natural
    yogurt, plus extra
    to serve
salt and pepper
boiled rice with chopped
    fresh parsley, to serve

Pork Stroganoff

Trim off any fat or gristle from the pork and cut into 1 cm/½ inch thick slices. Heat the vegetable oil in a large, heavy-based frying pan and gently fry the pork, onion and garlic for 4–5 minutes, or until lightly browned.

Stir in the flour and tomato purée, then pour in the chicken stock and stir to mix thoroughly. Add the mushrooms, green pepper, nutmeg and season to taste with salt and pepper. Bring to the boil, cover and simmer for 20 minutes, or until the pork is tender and cooked through.

Remove the frying pan from the heat and stir in the yogurt. Transfer the pork to 4 large, warmed serving plates and serve with boiled rice sprinkled with chopped fresh parsley and an extra spoonful of yogurt, garnished with freshly grated nutmeg.

SERVES 4

8 skinless, boneless chicken thighs, about 100 g/3½ oz each
2 tbsp sweet chilli dipping sauce
2 tbsp orange juice
2 garlic cloves, well crushed
salt and pepper

creole rice
600 ml/1 pint water
250 g/9 oz white long-grain rice
1 tbsp olive oil
1 large red pepper, deseeded and finely chopped

1 small onion, finely chopped
1 tsp paprika
400 g/14 oz canned mixed beans, drained and rinsed

Sweet Chilli Chicken with Creole Rice

Put the chicken in a shallow, non-metallic bowl. Mix the chilli sauce, orange juice and garlic together in a small bowl then season to taste with salt and pepper and spoon over the chicken. Using your hands, coat the chicken thighs thoroughly in the marinade. Cover and leave to marinate in the refrigerator for 1–2 hours.

Preheat the oven to 180°C/350°F/Gas Mark 4. Transfer the chicken thighs to a non-stick baking tray and bake in the preheated oven, turning halfway through, for 25 minutes, or until tender and the juices run clear when a skewer is inserted into the thickest part of the meat.

Meanwhile, make the rice. Lightly salt the water and bring to the boil in a saucepan. Add the rice and stir well. Cover, reduce the heat to low and leave to simmer, undisturbed, for 15 minutes, or until tender and all the water has been absorbed.

While the rice is cooking, heat the oil in a non-stick frying pan over a medium–high heat, add the red pepper and onion and cook, stirring frequently, for 10–15 minutes, or until the onion is thoroughly soft and turning golden, adding the paprika for the last 5 minutes of the cooking time. Stir in the beans and cook for a further 1 minute.

Stir the bean mixture into the rice, then serve immediately with the baked chicken.

SERVES 4

4 skinless, boneless chicken breasts, about 115 g/4 oz each
4 tbsp green olive tapenade

8 thin slices smoked pancetta
2 garlic cloves, chopped
250 g/9 oz cherry tomatoes, halved

100 ml/3½ fl oz dry white wine
2 tbsp olive oil
8 slices ciabatta
salt and pepper

Baked Tapenade Chicken

Preheat the oven to 220°C/425°F/Gas Mark 7. Place the chicken breasts on a board and cut three deep slashes into each. Spread a tablespoon of the tapenade over each chicken breast, pushing it into the slashes with a palette knife.

Wrap each chicken breast in two slices of pancetta. Place the chicken breasts in a shallow ovenproof dish and arrange the garlic and tomatoes around them. Season to taste with salt and pepper, then pour over the wine and 1 tablespoon of the oil. Bake in the preheated oven for about 20 minutes, until the juices run clear when the chicken is pierced with a skewer. Cover the dish loosely with foil and leave to stand for 5 minutes.

Meanwhile, preheat the grill to high. Brush the ciabatta with the remaining oil and cook under the preheated grill for 2–3 minutes, turning once, until golden.

Transfer the chicken and tomatoes to serving plates and spoon over the juices. Serve with the toasted ciabatta.

SERVES 4

55 g/2 oz butter
2 tbsp olive oil
1.8 kg/4 lb chicken pieces
115 g/4 oz rindless smoked bacon, cut into strips

115 g/4 oz baby onions
115 g/4 oz chestnut mushrooms, halved
2 garlic cloves, finely chopped
2 tbsp brandy
225 ml/8 fl oz red wine

300 ml/10 fl oz chicken stock
1 bouquet garni
2 tbsp plain flour
salt and pepper
chopped fresh flat-leaf parsley, to garnish

Coq au Vin

Melt half the butter with the olive oil in a large, flameproof casserole. Add the chicken and cook over a medium heat, stirring, for 8–10 minutes, or until golden brown all over. Add the bacon, onions, mushrooms and garlic. Pour in the brandy and set it alight with a match or taper. When the flames have died down, add the wine, stock and bouquet garni and season to taste with salt and pepper.

Bring to the boil, reduce the heat and simmer gently for 1 hour, or until the chicken pieces are cooked through and tender. Meanwhile, make a beurre manié by mashing the remaining butter with the flour in a small bowl.

Remove and discard the bouquet garni. Transfer the chicken to a large plate and keep warm. Stir the beurre manié into the casserole, a little at a time. Bring to the boil, stirring until thickened, then return the chicken to the casserole and serve immediately, garnished with the chopped parsley.

SERVES 4

3 tbsp olive oil
2.25 kg/5 lb chicken, cut into 8 pieces and dusted in flour
200 g/7 oz fresh chorizo sausages, roughly sliced
small bunch of sage leaves

1 onion, chopped
6 cloves garlic, sliced
2 sticks celery, sliced
1 small pumpkin/butternut squash, peeled and roughly chopped
200 ml/7 fl oz dry sherry

600 ml/1 pint chicken stock
400 g/14 oz chopped canned tomatoes
2 bay leaves
1 tbsp chopped fresh flat-leaf parsley
salt and pepper

Chicken, Pumpkin + Chorizo Casserole

Preheat the oven to 180°C/350°F/Gas Mark 4. Fry the chicken in the olive oil in a casserole with the chorizo and sage leaves, until golden brown. Remove with a slotted spoon and reserve. You may need to do this in two batches. Add the onion, garlic, celery and pumpkin to the casserole and cook for 20 minutes or until the mixture is golden brown.

Add the sherry, chicken stock, tomatoes and bay leaves, and season to taste with salt and pepper. Add the reserved chicken, chorizo and sage back into the casserole dish. Cover with a lid and cook in the oven for 1 hour.

Remove from the oven, stir in the chopped parsley and serve.

SERVES 4

1.8 kg/4 lb chicken
  pieces
2 tbsp sunflower oil
2 medium leeks
250 g/9 oz carrots,
  chopped
250 g/9 oz parsnips,
  chopped

2 small turnips, chopped
600 ml/1 pint chicken
  stock
3 tbsp Worcestershire
  sauce
2 sprigs fresh rosemary
salt and pepper

dumplings
200 g/7 oz self-raising
  flour
100 g/3½ oz suet
1 tbsp chopped
  rosemary leaves
cold water, to mix
salt and pepper

Chicken Casserole with Dumplings

Remove the skin from the chicken if you prefer. Heat the oil in a large, flameproof casserole or heavy saucepan and fry the chicken until golden. Using a slotted spoon, remove the chicken from the pan. Drain off the excess fat.

Trim and slice the leeks. Add the carrots, parsnips and turnips to the casserole and cook for 5 minutes, until lightly coloured. Return the chicken to the pan. Add the chicken stock, Worcestershire sauce, rosemary and season to taste with salt and pepper, then bring to the boil. Reduce the heat, cover and simmer gently for about 50 minutes or until the juices run clear when the chicken is pierced with a skewer.

To make the dumplings, combine the flour, suet, rosemary and seasoning in a bowl. Stir in just enough cold water to bind to a firm dough. Form into 8 small balls and place on top of the chicken and vegetables. Cover and simmer for a further 10–12 minutes, until the dumplings are well risen. Serve with the casserole.

SERVES 4

4 tbsp sunflower oil
900 g/2 lb chicken, chopped
250 g/9 oz mushrooms, sliced
16 shallots
6 garlic cloves, crushed
1 tbsp plain flour

250 ml/9 fl oz white wine
250 ml/9 fl oz chicken stock
1 bouquet garni (1 bay leaf, 1 fresh thyme sprig, 1 celery stick, 1 fresh parsley sprig and 1 fresh sage sprig, tied together with string)

400 g/14 oz canned borlotti beans
salt and pepper
freshly cooked squash, to serve

Garlic Chicken Casserole

Preheat the oven to 150°C/300°F/Gas Mark 2. Heat the oil in a large, flameproof casserole. Add the chicken and fry until browned all over. Remove the chicken from the casserole with a slotted spoon and reserve until required. Add the mushrooms, shallots and garlic to the casserole and cook for 4 minutes.

Return the chicken to the casserole and sprinkle with the flour, then cook for a further 2 minutes. Add the wine and stock, stir until boiling, then add the bouquet garni. Season to taste with salt and pepper. Drain the borlotti beans and rinse thoroughly, then add to the casserole.

Cover and place in the centre of the oven for 2 hours. Remove and discard the bouquet garni and serve the casserole with the squash.

SERVES 4

55 g/2 oz plain flour
4 turkey breast fillets,
   about 115 g/4 oz each
3 tbsp corn oil
1 onion, thinly sliced
1 red pepper, deseeded
   and sliced

300 ml/10 fl oz chicken
   stock
25 g/1 oz raisins
4 tomatoes, peeled,
   deseeded and
   chopped
1 tsp chilli powder
½ tsp ground cinnamon

pinch of ground cumin
25 g/1 oz plain
   chocolate, finely
   chopped or grated
salt and pepper
sprigs of fresh coriander,
   to garnish

Mexican Turkey

Preheat the oven to 160°C/325°F/Gas Mark 3. Spread the flour on a plate and season with salt and pepper. Coat the turkey fillets in the seasoned flour, shaking off any excess. Reserve any remaining seasoned flour.

Heat the oil in a flameproof casserole. Add the turkey fillets and cook over a medium heat, turning occasionally, for 5–10 minutes, or until golden. Transfer to a plate with a slotted spoon.

Add the onion and red pepper to the casserole. Cook over a low heat, stirring occasionally, for 5 minutes, or until softened. Sprinkle in the remaining seasoned flour and cook, stirring constantly, for 1 minute. Gradually stir in the stock, then add the raisins, chopped tomatoes, chilli powder, cinnamon, cumin and chocolate. Season to taste with salt and pepper. Bring to the boil, stirring constantly.

Return the turkey to the casserole, cover and cook in the preheated oven for 50 minutes. Serve immediately, garnished with sprigs of coriander.

SERVES 4

4 duck breasts, about 150 g/5½ oz each
2 tbsp olive oil
225 g/8 oz piece gammon, cut into small chunks
225 g/8 oz chorizo, outer casing removed and sliced
1 onion, chopped

3 garlic cloves, chopped
3 celery sticks, chopped
1–2 fresh red chillies, deseeded and chopped
1 green pepper, deseeded and chopped
600 ml/1 pint chicken stock

1 tbsp chopped fresh oregano
400 g/14 oz canned chopped tomatoes
1–2 tsp hot pepper sauce, or to taste
chopped fresh flat-leaf parsley, to garnish
green salad and freshly cooked rice, to serve

Duck Jambalaya-Style Stew

Remove and discard the skin and any fat from the duck breasts. Cut the flesh into bite-sized pieces.

Heat half the oil in a large deep frying pan and cook the duck, gammon and chorizo over a high heat, stirring frequently, for 5 minutes, or until browned on all sides and sealed. Using a slotted spoon, remove from the frying pan and set aside.

Add the onion, garlic, celery and chillies to the frying pan and cook over a medium heat, stirring frequently, for 5 minutes, or until softened. Add the green pepper, then stir in the stock, oregano, tomatoes and hot pepper sauce.

Bring to the boil, then reduce the heat and return the duck, gammon and chorizo to the frying pan. Cover and simmer, stirring occasionally, for 20 minutes, or until the duck and gammon are tender.

Serve immediately, garnished with parsley and accompanied by a green salad and rice.

Fish & Seafood

SERVES 4

8 monkfish fillets, weighing about 800 g/1 lb 12 oz in total
6 tbsp olive oil
1 onion, halved and thinly sliced into crescents

½ tsp finely chopped fresh rosemary
1 fresh red chilli, halved, deseeded and thinly sliced
3 tbsp capers, drained and rinsed
1 tbsp chopped flat-leaf parsley

coarsely grated zest of ½ lemon
250 ml/9 fl oz dry white wine
knob of butter
4 thin slices ciabatta or sourdough bread
salt and pepper

Baked Monkfish with Toasted Ciabatta

Preheat the oven to 200°C/400°F/Gas Mark 6. Remove any membrane from the monkfish fillets. Sprinkle with ½ teaspoon of salt and ¼ teaspoon of black pepper.

Heat 4 tablespoons of the olive oil in a flameproof baking dish or shallow casserole. Add the onion and rosemary, and fry over medium heat for 5 minutes until the onion is soft but not coloured. Add the chilli, capers, parsley and lemon zest, and fry for another 3 minutes until the onion is just beginning to colour. Pour in the wine, bring to the boil and simmer for 1 minute.

Remove the pan from the heat. Add the monkfish fillets in a single layer, spooning some of the onion mixture over the top. Bake in the oven for 20–25 minutes until the thickest part of the flesh looks opaque when pierced with the tip of a knife.

Transfer the fillets to a plate and keep warm. Bring the contents of the pan to the boil and simmer over medium–high heat for 2–3 minutes until the liquid is slightly reduced. Swirl in a knob of butter, taste and adjust the seasoning, if necessary.

Heat the remaining 2 tablespoons of olive oil in a frying pan. Add the slices of bread and fry for 1–2 minutes until golden on both sides.

Place a slice of bread on each serving plate. Arrange the monkfish fillets on top, and spoon over the sauce.

SERVES 8

1 kg/2 lb 4 oz selection of at least 4 different firm white fish fillets, such as red mullet, snapper, sea bass, eel or monkfish, scaled and cleaned, but not skinned
100 ml/3½ fl oz olive oil
2 onions, finely chopped

1 fennel bulb, finely chopped
4 garlic cloves, crushed
1.2 kg/2 lb 6 oz canned chopped plum tomatoes
1.5 litres/2¾ pints fish stock
pinch of saffron strands
grated zest of 1 orange

bouquet garni of 2 sprigs thyme, 2 sprigs parsley and 2 bay leaves, tied together with string
500 g/1 lb 2 oz mussels, cleaned
500 g/1 lb 2 oz cooked prawns, shell on
salt and pepper
French bread, to serve

Bouillabaisse

Carefully pin-bone the fish, then cut the fillets into bite-sized pieces.

Heat the olive oil in a very large frying pan or wide saucepan with a lid and gently fry the onion and fennel for about 15 minutes until soft. Add the garlic and fry for 2 minutes, then add the tomatoes and simmer for 2 minutes. Add the stock, saffron, orange zest and bouquet garni and bring to the boil. Simmer, uncovered, for 15 minutes.

Add the fish pieces, mussels and prawns and cover the pan. Simmer for a further 5–10 minutes, until the mussels have opened. Discard any that remain closed. Season to taste with salt and pepper.

Transfer to warmed bowls and serve with French bread.

SERVES 6

butter, plus extra for greasing
900 g/2 lb white fish fillets, such as plaice, skinned
150 ml/5 fl oz dry white wine
1 tbsp chopped fresh parsley, tarragon or dill

175 g/6 oz small mushrooms, sliced
100 g/3½ oz butter
175 g/6 oz cooked peeled prawns
40 g/1½ oz plain flour
125 ml/4 fl oz double cream

900 g/2 lb floury potatoes, peeled and cut into even-sized chunks
salt and pepper

Fisherman's Pie

Preheat the oven to 180°C/350°F/Gas Mark 4. Butter a 1.7-litre/3-pint baking dish. Fold the fish fillets in half and place in the dish. Season to taste with salt and pepper, pour over the wine and scatter over the herbs. Cover with foil and bake for 15 minutes until the fish starts to flake. Strain off the liquid and reserve for the sauce. Increase the oven temperature to 220°C/425°F/Gas Mark 7. Sauté the mushrooms in a frying pan with 15 g/½ oz of the butter and spoon over the fish. Scatter over the prawns.

Heat 55 g/2 oz of the butter in a saucepan and stir in the flour. Cook for a few minutes without browning, remove from the heat, then add the reserved cooking liquid gradually, stirring well between each addition. Return to the heat and gently bring to the boil, still stirring to ensure a smooth sauce. Add the cream and season to taste with salt and pepper. Pour over the fish in the dish and smooth over the surface.

Make the mashed potato by cooking the potatoes in boiling salted water for 15–20 minutes. Drain well and mash with a potato masher until smooth. Season to taste with salt and pepper and add the remaining butter, stirring until melted. Pile or pipe the potato onto the fish and sauce and bake for 10–15 minutes until golden brown. Serve immediately.

SERVES 4

200 g/7 oz squid, cleaned and tentacles discarded
500 g/1 lb 2 oz firm white fish fillets, preferably monkfish or halibut
1 tbsp corn oil
4 shallots, finely chopped
2 garlic cloves, finely chopped

2 tbsp Thai green curry paste
2 small lemon grass stems, finely chopped
1 tsp shrimp paste
500 ml/18 fl oz coconut milk
200 g/7 oz raw king prawns, peeled and deveined

12 live clams, scrubbed
8 fresh basil leaves, finely shredded, plus extra leaves to garnish
freshly cooked rice, to serve

Spicy Thai Seafood Stew

Using a sharp knife, cut the squid into thick rings and cut the fish into bite-sized chunks.

Preheat a large wok, then add the oil and heat. Add the shallots, garlic and curry paste and stir-fry for 1–2 minutes. Add the lemon grass and shrimp paste, then stir in the coconut milk and bring to the boil.

Reduce the heat until the liquid is simmering gently, then add the squid, fish and prawns and simmer for 2 minutes.

Discard any clams with broken shells and any that refuse to close when tapped. Add the clams and simmer for a further minute, or until the clams have opened. Discard any that remain closed. Sprinkle the shredded basil leaves over the stew.

Transfer to serving plates, garnish with basil leaves and serve immediately with freshly cooked rice.

SERVES 4

750 g/1 lb 10 oz squid
3 tbsp olive oil
1 onion, chopped
3 garlic cloves, finely
    chopped

1 tsp fresh thyme leaves
400 g/14 oz canned
    chopped tomatoes
150 ml/5 fl oz red wine
300 ml/10 fl oz water

1 tbsp chopped fresh
    parsley
salt and pepper
crusty bread, to serve

Squid Stew

To prepare whole squid, hold the body firmly and grasp the tentacles just inside the body. Pull firmly to remove the innards. Find the transparent quill and remove. Grasp the wings on the outside of the body and pull to remove the outer skin. Trim the tentacles just below the beak and reserve. Wash the body and tentacles under running water. Slice the body into rings. Drain well on kitchen paper.

Heat the oil in a large, flameproof casserole. Add the prepared squid and cook over a medium heat, stirring occasionally, until lightly browned.

Reduce the heat and add the onion, garlic and thyme. Cook, stirring occasionally, for a further 5 minutes until softened.

Stir in the tomatoes, red wine and water. Bring to the boil, then transfer the casserole to a preheated oven, 140°C/275°F/Gas Mark 1 for 2 hours. Stir in the parsley and season to taste with salt and pepper. Serve with crusty bread.

SERVES 4

1 yellow pepper, 1 red pepper, 1 orange pepper, deseeded and quartered
450 g/1 lb ripe tomatoes
2 large, fresh, mild green chillies, such as poblano
6 garlic cloves, peeled but kept whole
2 tsp dried oregano or dried mixed herbs

2 tbsp olive oil, plus extra for drizzling
1 large onion, finely chopped
450 ml/16 fl oz fish, vegetable or chicken stock
finely grated rind and juice of 1 lime
2 tbsp chopped fresh coriander, plus extra to garnish

1 bay leaf
450 g/1 lb red snapper fillets, skinned and cut into chunks
225 g/8 oz raw prawns, peeled and deveined
225 g/8 oz raw squid rings
salt and pepper
warmed flour tortillas, to serve

Seafood Stew

Preheat the oven to 200°C/400°F/Gas Mark 6. Put the pepper quarters, skin-side up, in a roasting tin with the tomatoes, chillies and garlic. Sprinkle with the oregano and drizzle with oil. Roast in the preheated oven for 30 minutes, or until the peppers are well browned and softened.

Remove the roasted vegetables from the oven and leave to stand until cool enough to handle. Peel off the skins from the peppers, tomatoes and chillies and chop the flesh. Finely chop the garlic.

Heat the oil in a large saucepan and cook the onion, stirring frequently, for 5 minutes, or until softened. Add the peppers, tomatoes, chillies, garlic, stock, lime rind and juice, coriander, bay leaf, and season to taste with salt and pepper. Bring to the boil, then stir in the seafood. Reduce the heat, cover and simmer gently for 10 minutes, or until the fish and squid are just cooked through and the prawns have turned pink. Remove and discard the bay leaf, then garnish with chopped coriander before serving accompanied by warmed flour tortillas.

SERVES 4

2 tbsp olive oil
2 red onions, finely
    chopped
1 garlic clove, crushed
2 courgettes, sliced
400 g/14 oz canned
    chopped tomatoes

850 ml/1½ pints fish or
    vegetable stock
85 g/3 oz dried pasta
    shapes
350 g/12 oz firm white
    fish, such as cod,
    haddock or hake

1 tbsp chopped fresh
    basil or oregano, plus
    extra to garnish
1 tsp grated lemon rind
1 tbsp cornflour
1 tbsp water
salt and pepper

Italian Fish Stew

Heat the oil in a large pan. Add the onions and garlic and cook over a low heat, stirring occasionally, for about 5 minutes, until softened. Add the courgettes and cook, stirring frequently, for 2–3 minutes.

Add the tomatoes and stock to the pan and bring to the boil. Add the pasta, bring back to the boil, reduce the heat and cover. Simmer for 5 minutes.

Skin and bone the fish, then cut it into chunks. Add to the pan with the basil and lemon rind and simmer gently for 5 minutes, until the fish is opaque and flakes easily (take care not to overcook it), and the pasta is tender but still firm to the bite.

Place the cornflour and water in a small bowl, mix to a smooth paste and stir into the stew. Cook gently for 2 minutes, stirring constantly, until thickened. Season to taste with salt and pepper.

Ladle the stew into 4 warmed soup bowls. Garnish with basil and serve immediately.

SERVES 4

2 tsp butter
1 large leek, thinly sliced
2 shallots, finely chopped
125 ml/4 fl oz dry cider
300 ml/10 fl oz fish stock
250 g/9 oz potatoes,
   diced

1 bay leaf
4 tbsp plain flour
200 ml/7 fl oz milk
200 ml/7 fl oz double
   cream
55 g/2 oz fresh sorrel
   leaves

350 g/12 oz skinless
   monkfish or cod fillet,
   cut into 2.5-cm/1-inch
   pieces
salt and pepper

Fish Stew with Cider

Melt the butter in a large saucepan over a medium–low heat. Add the leek and shallots and cook for about 5 minutes, stirring frequently, until they start to soften. Add the cider and bring to the boil.

Stir in the stock, potatoes and bay leaf with a large pinch of salt (unless the stock is salty) and bring back to the boil. Reduce the heat, cover and cook gently for 10 minutes.

Put the flour in a small bowl and very slowly whisk in a few tablespoons of the milk to make a thick paste. Stir in a little more to make a smooth liquid.

Adjust the heat so the stew bubbles gently. Stir in the flour mixture and cook, stirring frequently, for 5 minutes. Add the remaining milk and half the cream. Continue cooking for about 10 minutes until the potatoes are tender.

Finely chop the sorrel and combine with the remaining cream. Stir the sorrel cream into the stew and add the fish. Continue cooking, stirring occasionally, for about 3 minutes, until the monkfish stiffens. Taste the stew and adjust the seasoning, if necessary. Ladle into warmed bowls and serve.

SERVES 4–6

large pinch of saffron
  threads
4 tbsp almost-boiling
  water
6 tbsp olive oil
1 large onion, chopped
2 garlic cloves, finely
  chopped
1½ tbsp chopped fresh
  thyme leaves
2 bay leaves

2 red peppers, deseeded
  and roughly chopped
800 g/1 lb 12 oz canned
  chopped tomatoes
1 tsp smoked paprika
250 ml/9 fl oz fish stock
140 g/5 oz blanched
  almonds, toasted and
  finely ground
12–16 live mussels
12–16 live clams

600 g/1 lb 5 oz thick
  boned hake or cod
  fillets, skinned and
  cut into 5-cm/2-inch
  chunks
12–16 raw prawns,
  peeled and deveined
salt and pepper
thick crusty bread,
  to serve

Catalan Fish Stew

Put the saffron threads in a heatproof jug with the water and leave for at least
10 minutes to infuse.

Heat the oil in a large, heavy-based flameproof casserole over a medium–high
heat. Reduce the heat to low and cook the onion, stirring occasionally, for
10 minutes, or until golden but not browned. Stir in the garlic, thyme, bay leaves
and red peppers and cook, stirring frequently, for 5 minutes, or until the peppers
are softened and the onions have softened further. Add the tomatoes and paprika
and simmer, stirring frequently, for a further 5 minutes.

Stir in the stock, the saffron and its soaking liquid and the almonds and bring to the
boil, stirring. Reduce the heat and simmer for 5–10 minutes, until the sauce reduces
and thickens. Season to taste with salt and pepper.

Meanwhile, clean the mussels and clams by scrubbing or scraping the shells and
pulling out any beards that are attached to the mussels. Discard any with broken
shells or any that refuse to close when tapped.

Gently stir the hake into the stew so that it doesn't break up, then add the prawns,
mussels and clams. Reduce the heat to very low, cover and simmer for 5 minutes,
or until the hake is opaque, the mussels and clams have opened and the
prawns have turned pink. Discard any mussels or clams that remain closed. Serve
immediately with plenty of thick crusty bread for soaking up the juices.

SERVES 4–6

200 g/7 oz dried egg ribbon pasta, such as tagliatelle
25 g/1 oz butter
55 g/2 oz fine fresh breadcrumbs
400 ml/14 fl oz canned condensed cream of mushroom soup

125 ml/4 fl oz milk
2 celery sticks, chopped
1 red and 1 green pepper, deseeded and chopped
140 g/5 oz mature Cheddar cheese, roughly grated

2 tbsp chopped fresh parsley
200 g/7 oz canned tuna in oil, drained and flaked
salt and pepper

Tuna-Noodle Casserole

Preheat the oven to 200°C/400°F/Gas Mark 6. Bring a large saucepan of salted water to the boil. Add the pasta and cook for 2 minutes fewer than specified on the packet instructions.

Meanwhile, melt the butter in a separate, small saucepan over a medium heat. Stir in the breadcrumbs, then remove from the heat and reserve.

Drain the pasta well and reserve. Pour the soup into the pasta pan over a medium heat, then stir in the milk, celery, peppers, half the cheese and all the parsley. Add the tuna and gently stir in so that the flakes don't break up. Season to taste with salt and pepper. Heat just until small bubbles appear around the edge of the mixture – do not boil.

Stir the pasta into the pan and use 2 forks to mix all the ingredients together. Spoon the mixture into an ovenproof dish that is also suitable for serving and spread out. Stir the remaining cheese into the buttered breadcrumbs, then sprinkle over the top of the pasta mixture. Bake in the oven for 20–25 minutes until the topping is golden. Leave to stand for 5 minutes before serving straight from the dish.

SERVES 4

450 g/1 lb smoked haddock fillets, cut into 4 portions
600 ml/1 pint milk
2 tbsp butter, plus extra for greasing
2½ tbsp plain flour
pinch of freshly grated nutmeg

3 tbsp double cream
1 tbsp chopped fresh parsley
2 eggs, hard-boiled and mashed to a pulp
450 g/1 lb dried fusilli pasta
1 tbsp lemon juice

salt and pepper
fresh flat-leaved parsley, to garnish

to serve
boiled new potatoes
beetroot

Smoked Haddock Casserole

Generously grease a casserole with butter. Put the haddock in the casserole and pour over the milk. Bake in a preheated oven, 200°C/400°F/Gas Mark 6, for 15 minutes.

Carefully pour off the cooking liquid into a jug without breaking up the fish fillets and reserve. Leave the haddock in the casserole.

Melt the butter in a saucepan and stir in the flour. Gradually whisk in the reserved cooking liquid. Season to taste with salt, pepper and nutmeg. Stir in the cream, chopped parsley and mashed hard-boiled eggs and cook, stirring constantly, for 2 minutes.

Meanwhile, bring a large saucepan of lightly salted water to the boil. Add the fusilli and the lemon juice, bring back to the boil and cook for 8–10 minutes, until tender but still firm to the bite.

Drain the pasta and spoon or tip it over the fish. Top with the egg sauce and return the casserole to the oven for 10 minutes.

Transfer the casserole to serving plates, garnish with flat-leaved parsley and serve with boiled new potatoes and beetroot.

SERVES 4

2 tbsp olive oil
2 large onions, sliced into
  rings
3 garlic cloves, chopped

2 large courgettes, cut
  into sticks
3 tbsp fresh thyme, stalks
  removed
8 large sardine fillets

115 g/4 oz grated
  Parmesan cheese
4 eggs, beaten
300 ml/10 fl oz milk
salt and pepper

Fresh Baked Sardines

Heat 1 tablespoon of the olive oil in a frying pan. Add the onion rings and chopped garlic and fry over a low heat, stirring occasionally, for 2–3 minutes, until soft and translucent.

Add the courgettes to the pan and cook, stirring occasionally, for about 5 minutes, or until turning golden. Stir 2 tablespoons of the thyme leaves into the mixture and remove from the heat.

Place half the onions and courgettes in the base of a large ovenproof dish. Top with the sardine fillets and half the grated Parmesan cheese. Place the remaining onions and courgettes on top and sprinkle with the remaining thyme.

Mix the eggs and milk together in a bowl and season to taste with salt and pepper. Pour the mixture into the dish. Sprinkle the remaining Parmesan cheese over the top.

Bake in a preheated oven, 180°C/350°F/Gas Mark 4 for 20–25 minutes, or until golden and set. Serve the fresh baked sardines hot.

SERVES 4

2 tbsp olive oil
12 raw scallops, shelled, cleaned and halved
1 large onion, finely chopped
2 garlic cloves, well crushed
400 g/14 oz canned chopped tomatoes

2 tsp dried Herbes de Provence
150 ml/5 fl oz dry white wine
1 mild red chilli, deseeded and chopped (optional)
150 g/5½ oz cooked shelled mussels

200 g/7 oz large cooked, peeled prawns
pepper
2 tbsp chopped fresh parsley, to garnish

Seafood Provençale

Heat the oil in a large frying pan over a high heat, add the scallops and cook for 30 seconds on each side to sear. Remove with a fish slice and set aside.

Reduce the heat to medium, add the onion and cook for 8–10 minutes, or until soft and just turning golden.

Add the garlic and cook, stirring, for 1 minute, then add the tomatoes and their juice, herbs, wine, chilli, if using, and season to taste with pepper. Bring to a simmer and cook for 20 minutes.

Add the mussels and prawns to the frying pan with the scallops and gently simmer for a further 5 minutes.

Serve immediately, sprinkled with the parsley.

SERVES 4–6

350 g/12 oz mussels, scrubbed and debearded
4 tbsp olive oil
1 onion, finely chopped
1 green pepper, deseeded and chopped
2 garlic cloves, very finely chopped
5 tbsp tomato purée

1 tbsp chopped fresh flat-leaf parsley
1 tsp dried oregano
400 g/14 oz canned chopped tomatoes
225 ml/8 fl oz dry red wine
450 g/1 lb firm white fish, such as cod or monkfish, cut into 5-cm/2-inch pieces

115 g/4 oz scallops, halved
115 g/4 oz raw prawns, peeled and deveined
200 g/7 oz canned crabmeat
10–15 fresh basil leaves, shredded
salt and pepper

Seafood Hotpot with Red Wine & Tomatoes

Discard any mussels with broken shells and any that refuse to close when tapped.

Heat the oil in a heavy-based saucepan or flameproof casserole over a medium heat. Add the onion and green pepper and cook for 5 minutes, or until beginning to soften.

Stir in the garlic, tomato purée, parsley and oregano and cook for 1 minute, stirring.

Pour in the tomatoes and wine. Season to taste with salt and pepper.

Bring to the boil, then cover and simmer over a low heat for 30 minutes. Add the fish, cover and simmer for 15 minutes.

Add the mussels, scallops, prawns and crabmeat. Cover and cook for a further 15 minutes. Discard any mussels that remain closed. Stir in the basil just before serving.

SERVES 4

2 tbsp olive oil
1 onion, finely chopped
1 celery stick, finely
   chopped

115 g/4 oz green olives,
   stoned
450 g/1 lb tomatoes,
   chopped
3 tbsp bottled capers,
   drained

4 swordfish steaks, about
   140 g/5 oz each
salt and pepper
fresh flat-leaf parsley
   sprigs, to garnish

Mediterranean Swordfish

Heat the oil in a large, heavy-based frying pan. Add the onion and celery and cook over a low heat, stirring occasionally, for 5 minutes, or until softened.

Meanwhile, roughly chop half the olives. Stir the chopped and whole olives into the saucepan with the tomatoes and capers and season to taste with salt and pepper.

Bring to the boil, then reduce the heat, cover and simmer gently, stirring occasionally, for 15 minutes.

Add the swordfish steaks to the frying pan and return to the boil. Cover and simmer, turning the fish once, for 20 minutes, or until the fish is cooked and the flesh flakes easily. Transfer the fish to serving plates and spoon the sauce over them. Garnish with fresh parsley sprigs and serve immediately.

SERVES 4

2 tbsp olive oil
1 large onion, finely
   chopped
pinch of saffron threads
½ tsp ground cinnamon
1 tsp ground coriander
½ tsp ground cumin
½ tsp ground turmeric

200 g/7 oz canned
   chopped tomatoes
300 ml/10 fl oz fish stock
4 small red mullet,
   cleaned, boned
   and heads and tails
   removed
55 g/2 oz stoned green
   olives

1 tbsp chopped
   preserved lemon
3 tbsp chopped fresh
   coriander
salt and pepper
freshly cooked couscous,
   to serve

Moroccan Fish Tagine

Heat the olive oil in a flameproof casserole. Add the onion and cook gently over a very low heat, stirring occasionally, for 10 minutes, or until softened, but not coloured. Add the saffron, cinnamon, ground coriander, cumin and turmeric and cook for a further 30 seconds, stirring constantly.

Add the tomatoes and fish stock and stir well. Bring to the boil, reduce the heat, cover and simmer for 15 minutes. Uncover and simmer for 20–35 minutes, or until thickened.

Cut each red mullet in half, then add the fish pieces to the casserole, pushing them down into the liquid. Simmer the stew for a further 5–6 minutes, or until the fish is just cooked.

Carefully stir in the olives, preserved lemon and chopped coriander. Season to taste with salt and pepper and serve immediately with couscous.

SERVES 4

115 g/4 oz raw prawns, peeled and deveined
250 g/9 oz prepared scallops, thawed if frozen
115 g/4 oz monkfish fillet, cut into chunks
1 lime, peeled and thinly sliced
1 tbsp chilli powder
1 tsp ground cumin

3 tbsp chopped fresh coriander
2 garlic cloves, finely chopped
1 fresh green chilli, deseeded and chopped
3 tbsp corn oil
1 onion, roughly chopped
1 red and 1 yellow pepper, deseeded and chopped

½ tsp ground cloves
pinch of ground cinnamon
pinch of cayenne pepper
350 ml/12 fl oz fish stock
400 g/14 oz canned chopped tomatoes
400 g/14 oz canned red kidney beans, drained and rinsed
salt

Seafood Chilli

Place the prawns, scallops, monkfish chunks and lime slices in a large, non-metallic dish with ¼ teaspoon of the chilli powder, ¼ teaspoon of the ground cumin, 1 tablespoon of the chopped coriander, half the garlic, the fresh chilli and 1 tablespoon of the oil. Cover with clingfilm and leave to marinate for up to 1 hour.

Meanwhile, heat 1 tablespoon of the remaining oil in a flameproof casserole or large, heavy-based saucepan. Add the onion, the remaining garlic and the red and yellow peppers and cook over a low heat, stirring occasionally, for 5 minutes, or until softened.

Add the remaining chilli powder, the remaining cumin, the cloves, cinnamon and cayenne pepper, and the remaining oil, if needed, and season to taste with salt. Cook, stirring, for 5 minutes, then gradually stir in the stock and the tomatoes and their juices. Partially cover and simmer for 25 minutes.

Add the beans to the tomato mixture and spoon the fish and shellfish on top. Cover and cook for 10 minutes, or until the fish and shellfish are cooked through. Sprinkle with the remaining coriander and serve.

SERVES 6

2 tbsp sunflower or corn oil
175 g/6 oz okra, trimmed and cut into 2.5-cm/1-inch pieces
2 onions, finely chopped
4 celery sticks, very finely chopped
1 garlic clove, finely chopped

2 tbsp plain flour
½ tsp sugar
1 tsp ground cumin
700 ml/1¼ pints fish stock
1 red pepper and 1 green pepper, deseeded and chopped
2 large tomatoes, chopped

350 g/12 oz large raw prawns
4 tbsp chopped fresh parsley
1 tbsp chopped fresh coriander
dash of Tabasco sauce
350 g/12 oz cod or haddock fillets, skinned
350 g/12 oz monkfish fillet
salt and pepper

Louisiana Gumbo

Heat half the oil in a large, flameproof casserole, or large saucepan with tightly fitting lid, and cook the okra over a low heat, stirring frequently, for 5 minutes, or until browned. Using a slotted spoon, remove from the casserole and set aside.

Heat the remaining oil in the casserole and cook the onion and celery over a medium heat, stirring frequently, for 5 minutes, or until softened. Add the garlic and cook, stirring, for 1 minute. Sprinkle in the flour, sugar and cumin and season to taste with salt and pepper. Cook, stirring constantly, for 2 minutes, then remove from the heat.

Gradually stir in the stock and bring to the boil, stirring. Return the okra to the casserole and add the peppers and tomatoes. Partially cover, reduce the heat to very low and simmer gently, stirring occasionally, for 10 minutes. Meanwhile, peel and devein the prawns and reserve.

Add the herbs and Tabasco sauce to taste. Cut the cod and monkfish into 2.5-cm/1-inch chunks, then gently stir into the stew. Stir in the prawns. Cover and simmer gently for 5 minutes, or until the fish is cooked through and the prawns have turned pink. Transfer to a large, warmed serving dish and serve.

SERVES 4

2 tbsp vegetable oil
2 onions, roughly chopped
1 green pepper, deseeded and roughly chopped
2 celery sticks, roughly chopped
3 garlic cloves, finely chopped
2 tsp paprika

300 g/10½ oz skinless, boneless chicken breasts, chopped
100 g/3½ oz kabanos sausages, chopped
3 tomatoes, peeled and chopped
450 g/1 lb long-grain rice
850 ml/1½ pints hot chicken or fish stock

1 tsp dried oregano
2 bay leaves
12 large raw prawns, peeled and deveined
4 spring onions, finely chopped
2 tbsp chopped fresh parsley
salt and pepper
chopped fresh herbs, to garnish

Jambalaya

Heat the vegetable oil in a large frying pan over a low heat. Add the onions, green pepper, celery and garlic and cook for 8–10 minutes until all the vegetables have softened. Add the paprika and cook for a further 30 seconds. Add the chicken and sausages and cook for 8–10 minutes until lightly browned. Add the tomatoes and cook for 2–3 minutes until they have collapsed.

Add the rice to the pan and stir well. Pour in the hot stock, oregano and bay leaves and stir well. Cover and simmer for 10 minutes.

Add the prawns and stir. Cover again and cook for a further 6–8 minutes until the rice is tender and the prawns are cooked through.

Stir in the spring onions and parsley and season to taste with salt and pepper. Transfer to a large serving dish, garnish with chopped fresh herbs and serve.

SERVES 4

1 tbsp olive oil
55 g/2 oz butter
2 garlic cloves, chopped
350 g/12 oz risotto rice
1.3 litres/2¼ pints fish or
    chicken stock

250 g/9 oz mixed cooked
    seafood, such as
    prawns, squid, mussels
    and clams
2 tbsp chopped fresh
    oregano, plus extra
    to garnish

55 g/2 oz freshly grated
    pecorino or Parmesan
    cheese
salt and pepper

Seafood Risotto

Heat the oil with half of the butter in a deep saucepan over a medium heat until the butter has melted. Add the garlic and cook, stirring, for 1 minute.

Reduce the heat, add the rice and mix to coat in oil and butter. Cook, stirring constantly, for 2–3 minutes, or until the grains are translucent.

Gradually add the hot stock, a ladle at a time. Stir constantly and add more liquid as the rice absorbs each addition. Increase the heat to medium so that the liquid bubbles. Cook for 20 minutes, or until all the liquid is absorbed and the rice is creamy.

About 5 minutes before the rice is ready, add the seafood and oregano to the pan and mix well.

Remove the pan from the heat and season to taste with salt and pepper. Add the remaining butter and mix well, then stir in the grated cheese until it melts. Spoon onto warmed plates and serve immediately, garnished with the extra oregano.

SERVES 4

450 g/1 lb firm white fish fillets (such as cod or monkfish), skinned and cut into 2.5-cm/1-inch cubes
2 tsp ground cumin
2 tsp dried oregano
2 tbsp lime juice
150 ml/5 fl oz dark rum

1 tbsp dark muscovado sugar
3 garlic cloves, finely chopped
1 large onion, chopped
1 each medium red pepper, green pepper, yellow pepper, deseeded and sliced into rings

1.2 litres/2 pints fish stock
350 g/12 oz long-grain rice
salt and pepper
fresh oregano leaves and lime wedges, to garnish
crusty bread, to serve

Fish & Rice with Dark Rum

Place the cubes of fish in a bowl and add the cumin, oregano, lime juice, rum and sugar. Season to taste with salt and pepper. Mix thoroughly, cover with clingfilm and set aside to chill for 2 hours.

Meanwhile, place the garlic, onion and peppers in a large saucepan. Pour in the stock and stir in the rice. Bring to the boil, reduce the heat cover and simmer for 15 minutes.

Gently stir in the fish and the marinade juices. Bring back to the boil and simmer, uncovered, stirring occasionally but taking care not to break up the fish, for about 10 minutes until the fish is cooked through and the rice is tender.

Season to taste with salt and pepper and transfer to a warmed serving plate. Garnish with fresh oregano and lime wedges and serve with crusty bread.

SERVES 4

115 g/4 oz dried Chinese mushrooms
2 tbsp vegetable or groundnut oil
6 spring onions, chopped

55 g/2 oz desiccated coconut
1 fresh green chilli, deseeded and chopped
225 g/8 oz jasmine rice

150 ml/5 fl oz fish stock
400 ml/14 fl oz coconut milk
350 g/12 oz cooked peeled prawns
6 sprigs fresh Thai basil

Prawns with Coconut Rice

Place the mushrooms in a small bowl, cover with hot water and set aside to soak for 30 minutes. Drain, then cut off and discard the stalks and slice the caps.

Heat 1 tablespoon of the oil in a wok and stir-fry the spring onions, coconut and chilli for 2–3 minutes, until lightly browned. Add the mushrooms and stir-fry for 3–4 minutes.

Add the rice and stir-fry for 2–3 minutes, then add the stock and bring to the boil. Lower the heat and add the coconut milk. Simmer for 10–15 minutes, until the rice is tender. Stir in the prawns and basil, heat through and serve.

SERVES 4–6

675 g/1 lb 8 oz prepared squid
3 tbsp olive oil
1 onion, finely chopped
3 garlic cloves, finely chopped

½ tsp thyme leaves
7 tbsp chopped flat leaf parsley
125 ml/4 fl oz white wine
250 g/9 oz canned chopped tomatoes

3 medium potatoes, about 450 g/1 lb in total, cut into bite-sized chunks
grated zest of 1 lemon
salt and pepper

Braised Squid with Potatoes, Lemon & Parsley

Slice the body of the squid crossways into thin rings. Cut the rings in half if large. Slice the tentacles and wings into bite-sized pieces.

Heat a heavy-based casserole over medium heat, add the oil and gently fry the onion for about 10 minutes until golden. Stir in the garlic, thyme and 3 tablespoons of the parsley.

Add the squid and cook for 2–3 minutes, stirring, until opaque. Pour in the wine and simmer for 2 minutes, then add the tomatoes and ¼ teaspoon of pepper. Bring to the boil, then cover and simmer gently for 1–1½ hours until the squid is tender. Stir occasionally to prevent sticking, adding a little water if necessary.

Add the potatoes to the casserole, and season to taste with salt and pepper. Cover and simmer for 20–30 minutes, or until the potatoes are tender but not breaking up.

Combine the lemon zest with the remaining parsley, and add to the casserole just before serving.

SERVES 4

85 g/3 oz sultanas
5 tbsp olive oil
6 tbsp chopped fresh
  flat-leaf parsley, plus
  extra to garnish

2 garlic cloves, finely
  chopped
800 g/1 lb 12 oz
  prepared squid, sliced,
  or squid rings
125 ml/4 fl oz dry white
  wine

500 g/1 lb 2 oz passata
pinch of chilli powder
85 g/3 oz pine kernels,
  finely chopped
salt

Squid with Parsley & Pine Kernels

Place the sultanas in a small bowl, cover with lukewarm water and set aside for 15 minutes to plump up.

Meanwhile, heat the olive oil in a heavy-based saucepan. Add the parsley and garlic and cook over a low heat, stirring frequently, for 3 minutes. Add the squid and cook, stirring occasionally, for 5 minutes.

Increase the heat to medium, pour in the wine and cook until it has almost completely evaporated. Stir in the passata and season to taste with chilli powder and salt. Lower the heat, cover and simmer gently, stirring occasionally, for 45–50 minutes, until the squid is almost tender.

Drain the sultanas and stir them into the saucepan with the pine kernels. Leave to simmer for a further 10 minutes, then serve immediately, garnished with chopped parsley.

SERVES 4

2 kg/4 lb 8 oz live mussels
300 ml/10 fl oz dry white
  wine

6 shallots, finely chopped
1 bouquet garni
pepper

4 bay leaves, to garnish
crusty bread, to serve

Moules Marinière

Clean the mussels by scrubbing or scraping the shells and pulling off any beards. Discard any with broken shells or any that refuse to close when tapped. Rinse the mussels under cold running water.

Pour the wine into a large, heavy-based saucepan, add the shallots and bouquet garni and season to taste with pepper. Bring to the boil over a medium heat. Add the mussels, cover tightly and cook, shaking the saucepan occasionally, for 5 minutes. Remove and discard the bouquet garni and any mussels that remain closed. Divide the mussels between 4 serving bowls with a slotted spoon. Tilt the pan to let any sand settle, then spoon the cooking liquid over the mussels, garnish with a bay leaf, and serve immediately with crusty bread.

Vegetarian

SERVES 6

2 tbsp olive oil
8 baby onions, peeled
2 celery stalks, sliced
225 g/8 oz carrots, thickly
 sliced
225 g/8 oz turnips, diced

55 g/2 oz pearl barley,
 rinsed
700–850 ml/1¼–1½ pints
 vegetable stock
350 g/12 oz chicken-style
 meat-free substitute,
 diced

85 g/3 oz partially
 thawed frozen peas
salt and pepper
1 tbsp chopped fresh
 parsley, to garnish

Vegetable Pot

Preheat the oven to 180°C/350°F/Gas Mark 4. Heat half the oil in a large saucepan or flameproof casserole dish over a medium heat, add the onions, celery, carrots and turnips and cook for 10 minutes, stirring frequently. Add the pearl barley and cook for 1 minute, stirring occasionally, then pour in the stock and bring to the boil.

If necessary, transfer to an ovenproof casserole dish. Season to taste with salt and pepper and cover. Cook in the preheated oven for 1–1¼ hours.

Meanwhile, heat the remaining oil in a frying pan over a medium heat, add the chicken-style pieces and cook, stirring frequently, for 5–8 minutes, or until golden.

Add the chicken-style pieces to the casserole with the peas and cook for a further 10–20 minutes, or until the vegetables are tender. Taste and adjust the seasoning, if necessary, and serve sprinkled with parsley.

SERVES 4

4 tbsp olive oil
1 tsp cumin seeds, crushed
1 onion, halved lengthways and finely sliced into crescents
3 garlic cloves, finely chopped

½ fresh red chilli, deseeded and thinly sliced
450 g/1 lb green beans, trimmed and halved
650 g/1 lb 7 oz canned chopped tomatoes and juice

400 g/14 oz canned chickpeas, drained and rinsed
finely grated zest of ½ lemon
3 tbsp chopped flat leaf parsley
salt and pepper
warm pita bread, to serve

Spicy Green Beans, Chickpeas & Tomatoes

Heat a heavy-based casserole over medium heat. Add the oil and cumin seeds, and sizzle for a few seconds to flavour the oil. Add the onion, reduce the heat to medium–low, and simmer for 10 minutes until starting to colour. Stir in the garlic and chilli and cook for another minute.

Add the beans, increase the heat to medium, and stir for 3 minutes until the beans are glossy and bright green. Season to taste with salt and pepper.

Stir in the tomatoes and chickpeas. Bring to the boil, then reduce the heat and simmer, covered, for 30–40 minutes, or until the beans are tender but not mushy. Check the seasoning, and stir in the lemon zest and parsley.

Serve hot, warm or at room temperature with plenty of warm pita bread to mop up the juices.

SERVES 4

150 ml/5 fl oz olive oil
2 onions, sliced
2 garlic cloves, finely chopped
2 medium-sized aubergines, roughly chopped

4 courgettes, roughly chopped
2 yellow peppers, deseeded and chopped
2 red peppers, deseeded and chopped

1 bouquet garni,
3 large tomatoes, peeled, deseeded and roughly chopped
salt and pepper

Classic Ratatouille

Heat the oil in a large saucepan. Add the onions and cook over a low heat, stirring occasionally, for 5 minutes, or until softened. Add the garlic and cook, stirring frequently for a further 2 minutes.

Add the aubergines, courgettes and peppers. Increase the heat to medium and cook, stirring occasionally, until the peppers begin to colour. Add the bouquet garni, reduce the heat, cover and simmer gently for 40 minutes.

Stir in the chopped tomatoes and season to taste with salt and pepper. Re-cover the saucepan and simmer gently for a further 10 minutes. Remove and discard the bouquet garni. Serve warm or cold.

SERVES 4

- 2 tbsp olive oil
- 1 large Spanish onion, sliced
- 2 peppers, any colour, deseeded and thinly sliced
- 2 courgettes, sliced into thin rounds
- 1 small aubergine, halved lengthways and thinly sliced
- 2 garlic cloves, chopped
- 300 ml/10 fl oz passata with herbs, plus extra if needed
- 2 tsp smoked paprika
- 8 small eggs
- salt and pepper

Ratatouille with Poached Eggs

Heat the oil in a large, lidded, non-stick frying pan or shallow, flameproof casserole over a medium–high heat, add the onion and peppers and cook, stirring frequently, for 4–5 minutes until beginning to soften.

Add the courgettes, aubergine and garlic and cook, stirring, for 2 minutes. Add the passata, most of the paprika and season to taste with salt and pepper. Stir and bring to a simmer. Reduce the heat to low, cover and leave to simmer gently for 45 minutes, adding a little extra passata or water if the mixture begins to look dry.

Make 8 wells in the ratatouille and break an egg into each. Re-cover and cook for a further 10 minutes, or until the egg whites are cooked but the yolks still runny.

Serve immediately, garnished with paprika.

SERVES 4

1 tbsp olive oil
1 red onion, halved and sliced
3 garlic cloves, crushed
225 g/8 oz spinach leaves
1 fennel bulb, cut into eighths

1 red pepper, deseeded and diced
1 tbsp plain flour
450 ml/16 fl oz vegetable stock
85 ml/3 fl oz dry white wine

400 g/14 oz canned chickpeas, drained
1 bay leaf
1 tsp ground coriander
½ tsp paprika
salt and pepper
fennel fronds, to garnish

Chickpea & Vegetable Casserole

Heat the oil in a large, flameproof casserole. Add the onion and garlic and sauté for 1 minute, stirring. Add the spinach and cook for 4 minutes, or until wilted.

Add the fennel and pepper and cook for 2 minutes, stirring. Stir in the flour and cook for 1 minute. Add the stock, wine, chickpeas, bay leaf, coriander and paprika, cover and cook for 30 minutes. Remove and discard the bay leaf. Season to taste with salt and pepper, garnish with fennel fronds and serve immediately.

SERVES 4–8

500 g/1 lb 2 oz large flat
  mushrooms
2 tbsp oil
1 onion, sliced
1 red pepper, deseeded
  and sliced

1 green pepper,
  deseeded and sliced
1 garlic clove, crushed
¼–½ tsp cayenne pepper
juice and grated rind of
  2 limes

2 tsp sugar
1 tsp dried oregano
8 flour tortillas
salt and pepper
salsa, to serve

Mushroom Fajitas

Cut the mushrooms into strips. Heat the oil in a large, heavy-based frying pan.
Add the mushrooms, onion, red and green pepper and garlic and stir-fry for
8–10 minutes, until the vegetables are cooked.

Add the cayenne pepper, lime juice and rind, sugar and oregano. Season to taste
with salt and pepper and cook for a further 2 minutes.

Meanwhile, heat the tortillas according to the packet instructions. Divide the
mushroom mixture between the warmed tortillas and serve with the salsa.

SERVES 4

100 ml/3½ fl oz olive oil
2 red onions, cut into
    8 wedges
3 garlic cloves, crushed
2 tsp ground cumin
2 tsp ground coriander

pinch of cayenne pepper
1 carrot, thickly sliced
2 small turnips, quartered
1 courgette, sliced
500 g/1 lb 2 oz potatoes,
    thickly sliced

juice and grated rind of
    2 large lemons
300 ml/10 fl oz vegetable
    stock
2 tbsp chopped fresh
    coriander
salt and pepper

Potato & Lemon Casserole

Heat the olive oil in a flameproof casserole. Add the onions and sauté over a medium heat, stirring frequently, for 3 minutes.

Add the garlic and cook for 30 seconds. Stir in the ground cumin, ground coriander and cayenne and cook, stirring constantly, for 1 minute.

Add the carrot, turnips, courgette and potatoes and stir to coat in the oil.

Add the lemon juice and rind and the stock. Season to taste with salt and pepper. Cover and cook over a medium heat, stirring occasionally, for 20–30 minutes until tender.

Remove the lid, sprinkle in the chopped fresh coriander and stir well. Serve immediately.

SERVES 4

1 tbsp olive oil, for
 brushing
680 g/1 lb 8 oz potatoes,
 peeled and thinly
 sliced

2 leeks, trimmed and
 sliced
2 beef tomatoes, sliced
8 fresh basil leaves

1 garlic clove, finely
 chopped
150 ml/5 fl oz vegetable
 stock
salt and pepper

Layered Vegetable Casserole

Preheat the oven to 180°C/350°F/Gas Mark 4. Brush a large flameproof casserole with a little of the olive oil.

Place a layer of potato slices in the bottom of the casserole and cover with a layer of leeks. Top with a layer of tomato slices and a few basil leaves. Repeat these layers until all the vegetables are used up, ending with a layer of potatoes. Stir the chopped garlic into the vegetable stock and season to taste with salt and pepper. Pour the stock over the vegetables and brush the top with the remaining oil.

Bake in the centre of the preheated oven for 1½ hours, or until the vegetables are tender and the topping is golden and brown. Serve immediately.

SERVES 4-6

1 onion, sliced
2 leeks, washed and sliced
2 sticks celery, chopped
2 carrots, thinly sliced
1 red pepper, seeded and sliced

225 g/8 oz prepared pumpkin flesh (peeled and seeded weight), diced
450 g/1 lb mixed root vegetables, such as sweet potato, parsnip and swede (prepared weight), diced

400 g/14 oz canned chopped tomatoes
150–200 ml/5-7 fl oz dry cider
2 tsp dried Herbes de Provence
salt and pepper
chopped fresh herbs, to garnish

Root Vegetable & Pumpkin Casserole

Preheat the oven to 180°C/350°F/Gas Mark 4. Place the onion, leeks, celery, carrots, pepper, diced pumpkin and root vegetables in a large, ovenproof casserole dish and mix well. Stir in the tomatoes, 150 ml/¼ pint of the cider, the dried herbs and season to taste with salt and pepper.

Cover and bake in the centre of the oven for 1¼–1½ hours or until the vegetables are cooked through and tender, stirring once or twice and adding a little extra cider, if desired. Garnish with a sprinkling of chopped fresh herbs and serve.

SERVES 4

225 g/8 oz red lentils
55 g/2 oz long-grain rice
1.2 litres/2 pints
  vegetable stock
1 leek, cut into chunks
3 garlic cloves, crushed
400 g/14 oz canned
  chopped tomatoes

1 tsp ground cumin
1 tsp chilli powder
1 tsp garam masala
1 red pepper, deseeded
  and sliced
100 g/3½ oz small
  broccoli florets
8 baby sweetcorn, halved
  lengthways

55 g/2 oz French beans,
  halved
1 tbsp shredded fresh
  basil
salt and pepper
fresh basil sprigs,
  to garnish

Lentil + Rice Casserole

Place the lentils, rice and stock in a large flameproof casserole and cook over a
low heat, stirring occasionally, for 20 minutes.

Add the leek, garlic, tomatoes and their can juice, ground cumin, chilli powder,
garam masala, red pepper, broccoli, baby sweetcorn and French beans to the pan.

Bring the mixture to the boil, reduce the heat, cover and simmer for a further
10–15 minutes or until the vegetables are tender. Add the shredded basil and
season to taste with salt and pepper. Garnish with fresh basil sprigs and serve
immediately.

SERVES 4

450 g/1 lb potatoes
1 leek, sliced
3 garlic cloves, crushed
50 g/1¾ oz Cheddar
  cheese, grated

50 g/1¾ oz mozzarella
  cheese, grated
25 g/1 oz freshly grated
  Parmesan cheese
2 tbsp chopped fresh
  flat-leaf parsley, plus
  extra to garnish

150 ml/5 fl oz single
  cream
150 ml/5 fl oz milk
salt and pepper

Cheese & Potato Layered Casserole

Preheat the oven to 160°C/325°F/Gas Mark 3. Cook the potatoes in a saucepan of lightly salted boiling water for 10 minutes. Drain well.

Cut the potatoes into thin slices. Arrange a layer of potatoes in the base of an ovenproof dish. Layer with a little of the leek, garlic, cheeses and chopped parsley and season well with salt and pepper.

Repeat the layers until all of the ingredients have been used, finishing with a layer of cheese on top.

Mix the cream and milk together, season to taste with salt and pepper and pour the mixture over the potato layers. Cook in the oven for 1–1¼ hours, or until the cheese is golden brown and bubbling and the potatoes are cooked through. Garnish with chopped parsley and serve immediately.

SERVES 4

450 g/1 lb cauliflower, broken into florets
2 large potatoes, cubed
100 g/3½ oz cherry tomatoes

sauce
25 g/1 oz butter or margarine
1 leek, sliced
1 garlic clove, crushed
25 g/1 oz plain flour
300 ml/10 fl oz milk

75 g/2¾ oz mixed grated cheese, such as Cheddar, Parmesan and Gruyère
½ tsp paprika
2 tbsp chopped fresh flat-leaf parsley, plus extra to garnish
salt and pepper

Cauliflower Bake

Preheat the oven to 180°C/350°F/Gas Mark 4. Cook the cauliflower in a saucepan of boiling water for 10 minutes. Drain well and reserve. Meanwhile, cook the potatoes in a separate saucepan of boiling water for 10 minutes, drain and reserve.

To make the sauce, melt the butter or margarine in a saucepan. Add the leek and garlic and sauté for 1 minute. Add the flour and cook for 1 minute. Remove the saucepan from the heat and gradually stir in the milk, 50 g/1¾ oz of the cheese, the paprika and parsley. Return the saucepan to the heat. Bring to the boil, stirring. Season to taste with salt and pepper.

Spoon the cauliflower into a deep, ovenproof dish. Add the tomatoes and top with the potatoes. Pour the sauce over the potatoes and sprinkle over the remaining cheese.

Cook in the oven for 20 minutes, or until the vegetables are cooked through and the cheese is golden brown and bubbling. Garnish with parsley and serve immediately.

SERVES 2

4 tbsp olive oil
2 onions, finely chopped
2 garlic cloves, very finely
   chopped
2 aubergines, thickly
   sliced

3 tbsp chopped fresh
   flat-leaf parsley
½ tsp dried thyme
400 g/14 oz canned
   chopped tomatoes

175 g/6 oz mozzarella,
   coarsely grated
6 tbsp freshly grated
   Parmesan cheese
salt and pepper

Aubergine Gratin

Heat the oil in a flameproof casserole over a medium heat. Add the onion and cook for 5 minutes, or until soft. Add the garlic and cook for a few seconds, or until just beginning to colour. Using a slotted spoon, transfer the onion mixture to a plate.

Cook the aubergine slices in batches in the same flameproof casserole until they are just lightly browned. Transfer to another plate.

Preheat the oven to 200°C/400°F/Gas Mark 6. Arrange a layer of aubergine slices in the base of the casserole dish or a shallow ovenproof dish. Sprinkle with some of the parsley, thyme and season to taste with salt and pepper. Add layers of onion, tomatoes and mozzarella, sprinkling parsley, thyme and seasoning over each layer.

Continue layering, finishing with a layer of aubergine slices. Sprinkle with the Parmesan. Bake, uncovered, in the preheated oven for 20–30 minutes, or until the top is golden and the aubergines are tender. Serve hot.

SERVES 4-6

55 g/2 oz unsalted butter, plus extra for greasing
6 courgettes, sliced
200 g/7 oz Gruyère or Parmesan cheese, grated

2 tbsp chopped fresh tarragon or a mixture of mint, tarragon and flat-leaf parsley
125 ml/4 fl oz milk

125 ml/4 fl oz double cream
2 eggs
freshly grated nutmeg
salt and pepper

Courgette & Cheese Gratin

Melt the butter in a large sauté pan or frying pan over a medium–high heat. Add the courgettes and sauté for 4–6 minutes, turning the slices over occasionally, until coloured on both sides. Remove from the pan and drain on kitchen paper, then season with salt and pepper.

Spread half the courgettes over the bottom of a greased ovenproof serving dish. Sprinkle with 55 g/2 oz of the cheese and half the herbs. Repeat these layers once more.

Mix the milk, cream and eggs together and season to taste with nutmeg, salt and pepper. Pour this liquid over the courgettes, then sprinkle the top with the remaining cheese.

Bake the gratin in a preheated oven, 180°C/350°F/Gas Mark 4, for 35–45 minutes, or until it is set in the centre and golden brown. Remove from the oven and let stand for 5 minutes before serving straight from the dish.

SERVES 4

1 cauliflower, cut into
    florets
55 g/2 oz butter
115 g/4 oz button
    mushrooms, sliced
salt and pepper

topping
115 g/4 oz dry
    breadcrumbs
2 tbsp grated Parmesan
    cheese

1 tsp dried oregano
1 tsp dried parsley
25 g/1 oz butter

Mushroom + Cauliflower Cheese Crumble

Bring a large saucepan of lightly salted water to the boil. Add the cauliflower and cook for 3 minutes. Remove from the heat, drain well and transfer to a shallow ovenproof dish.

Preheat the oven to 230°C/450°F/Gas Mark 8. Melt the butter in a small frying pan over a medium heat. Add the mushrooms, stir and cook gently for 3 minutes. Remove from the heat and spoon on top of the cauliflower. Season to taste with salt and pepper. For the topping, combine the breadcrumbs, Parmesan and herbs in a small mixing bowl, then sprinkle over the vegetables.

Dice the butter and dot over the breadcrumb mixture. Bake in the preheated oven for 15 minutes, or until the topping is golden brown. Serve straight from the cooking dish.

SERVES 4-6

3 parsnips, weighing about 650 g/1 lb 7 oz in total

4 large carrots, weighing about 400 g/14 oz in total

butter, for greasing

400 ml/14 fl oz chicken or vegetable stock

400 ml/14 fl oz double cream

2 large garlic cloves, flattened with a knife blade

freshly grated nutmeg

salt and pepper

Peppery Parsnip & Carrot Gratin

Preheat the oven to 180°C/350°F/Gas Mark 4. Slice the parsnips and carrots, and place in a steamer basket set over boiling water. Steam for 3–4 minutes until tender. Butter a large ovenproof baking dish and arrange the vegetables in it.

Heat the stock and cream in a saucepan with the garlic. Season with two good pinches of grated nutmeg and season to taste with salt and pepper.

Pour the hot cream mixture over the vegetables. Cover the dish with foil and bake for 30 minutes. Remove the foil and bake for another 20–25 minutes, or until golden on top. Sprinkle with a little more nutmeg and pepper before serving.

SERVES 4

1 large fennel bulb
2 tbsp olive oil
1 red onion, cut into small wedges
2–4 garlic cloves, sliced
1 fresh green chilli, deseeded and chopped
1 small aubergine, about 225 g/8 oz, cut into chunks

2 tbsp tomato purée
600 ml/1 pint vegetable stock
450 g/1 lb ripe tomatoes
1 tbsp balsamic vinegar
a few sprigs fresh oregano
400 g/14 oz canned borlotti beans
400 g/14 oz canned flageolet beans

1 yellow pepper, deseeded and cut into small strips
1 courgette, sliced into half moons
55 g/2 oz stoned black olives
25 g/1 oz Parmesan cheese, freshly shaved
salt and pepper
crusty bread, to serve

Tuscan Bean Stew

Trim the fennel and reserve any feathery fronds, then cut the bulb into small strips. Heat the oil in a large, heavy-based saucepan with a tight-fitting lid, and cook the onion, garlic, chilli and the fennel strips, stirring frequently, for 5–8 minutes, or until softened.

Add the aubergine and cook, stirring frequently, for 5 minutes. Blend the tomato purée with a little of the stock in a jug and pour over the fennel mixture, then add the remaining stock, and the tomatoes, vinegar and oregano. Bring to the boil, then reduce the heat, cover and simmer for 15 minutes, or until the tomatoes have begun to collapse.

Drain and rinse the beans, the drain again. Add them to the pan with the yellow pepper, courgette and olives. Simmer for a further 15 minutes, or until all the vegetables are tender. Taste and adjust the seasoning, if necessary. Scatter with the Parmesan cheese shavings and serve garnished with the reserved fennel fronds, accompanied by crusty bread.

SERVES 6

1 tbsp olive oil
1 onion, finely chopped
1 garlic clove, finely
   chopped
1 carrot, halved and
   thinly sliced

450 g/1 lb young green
   cabbage, cored,
   quartered and thinly
   sliced
400 g/14 oz canned
   chopped tomatoes
½ tsp dried thyme
2 bay leaves

1.5 litres/2¾ pints chicken
   or vegetable stock
200 g/7 oz Puy lentils
450 ml/16 fl oz water
salt and pepper
chopped fresh parsley,
   to garnish

Vegetable Stew with Green Lentils

Heat the oil in a large saucepan over a medium heat, add the onion, garlic and carrot and cook for 3–4 minutes, stirring frequently, until the onion starts to soften. Add the cabbage and cook for a further 2 minutes.

Add the tomatoes, thyme and 1 bay leaf, then pour in the stock. Bring to the boil, reduce the heat to low and cook gently, partially covered, for about 45 minutes until the vegetables are tender. Remove and discard the bay leaf.

Meanwhile, put the lentils in another saucepan with the remaining bay leaf and the water. Bring just to the boil, reduce the heat and simmer for about 25 minutes until tender. Drain off any remaining water, and set aside.

Allow the stew to cool, then transfer to a food processor or blender and process until smooth, working in batches, if necessary. (If using a food processor, strain off the cooking liquid and reserve. Purée the solids with enough cooking liquid to moisten them, then combine with the remaining liquid.)

Return the stew to the saucepan, remove and discard the bay leaf and add the cooked lentils. Taste and adjust the seasoning, if necessary, and cook for about 10 minutes to heat through. Ladle into warmed bowls and garnish with parsley.

SERVES 4

4 garlic cloves
1 small acorn squash
1 red onion, sliced
2 leeks, sliced
1 aubergine, sliced
1 small celeriac, diced
2 turnips, sliced
2 plum tomatoes, chopped
1 carrot, sliced

1 courgette, sliced
2 red peppers
1 fennel bulb, sliced
175 g/6 oz chard
2 bay leaves
½ tsp fennel seeds
½ tsp chilli powder
pinch each of dried thyme, dried oregano and sugar

125 ml/4 fl oz extra virgin olive oil
225 ml/8 fl oz vegetable stock
25 g/1 oz fresh basil leaves, torn
4 tbsp chopped fresh parsley
salt and pepper
2 tbsp freshly grated Parmesan cheese, to serve

Italian Vegetable Stew

Finely chop the garlic and dice the squash. Put them in a large, heavy-based saucepan with a tight-fitting lid. Add the onion, leeks, aubergine, celeriac, turnips, tomatoes, carrot, courgette, red peppers, fennel, chard, bay leaves, fennel seeds, chilli powder, thyme, oregano, sugar, oil, stock and half the basil. Mix together well, then bring to the boil.

Reduce the heat, cover and simmer for 30 minutes, or until all the vegetables are tender.

Sprinkle in the remaining basil and the parsley and season to taste with salt and pepper. Remove and discard the bay leaves. Serve immediately, sprinkled with the cheese.

SERVES 4

1 tbsp olive oil
1 garlic clove, crushed
8 small onions, halved
2 celery sticks, sliced
225 g/8 oz swede, chopped
2 carrots, sliced
½ small head of cauliflower, broken into florets
225 g/8 oz button mushrooms, sliced

400 g/14 oz canned chopped tomatoes
55 g/2 oz red lentils, rinsed
2 tbsp cornflour
3–4 tbsp water
300 ml/10 fl oz vegetable stock
2 tsp Tabasco sauce
2 tsp chopped fresh oregano
fresh oregano sprigs, to garnish

topping

225 g/8 oz self-raising flour
pinch of salt
4 tbsp butter
115 g/4 oz grated mature Cheddar cheese
2 tsp chopped fresh oregano
1 egg, lightly beaten
150 ml/5 fl oz milk

Winter Vegetable Cobbler

Preheat the oven to 180°C/350°F/Gas Mark 4. Heat the oil in a large frying pan and cook the garlic and onions over a low heat for 5 minutes. Add the celery, swede, carrots and cauliflower and cook for 2–3 minutes.

Add the mushrooms, tomatoes and lentils. Place the cornflour and water in a bowl and mix to make a smooth paste. Stir into the frying pan with the stock, Tabasco and oregano. Transfer to an ovenproof dish, cover and bake in the preheated oven for 20 minutes.

To make the topping, sift the flour and salt into a bowl. Add the butter and rub it in, then stir in most of the cheese and oregano. Beat the egg with the milk in a small bowl and add enough to the dry ingredients to make a soft dough. Knead, then roll out on a lightly floured work surface to 1 cm/½ inch thick. Cut into 5-cm/2-inch rounds.

Remove the dish from the oven and increase the temperature to 200°C/400°F/Gas Mark 6. Arrange the dough rounds around the edge of the dish, brush with the remaining egg and milk mixture and sprinkle with the reserved cheese. Cook for a further 10–12 minutes. Garnish with oregano sprigs and serve.

SERVES 4

15 g/½ oz sun-dried tomatoes, chopped
225 g/8 oz Puy lentils
600 ml/1 pint cold water
2 tbsp olive oil
½–1 tsp crushed dried chillies
2–3 garlic cloves, chopped
1 large onion, cut into small wedges

1 small celeriac, cut into small chunks
225 g/8 oz carrots, sliced
225 g/8 oz new potatoes, scrubbed and cut into chunks
1 small acorn squash, deseeded, peeled and cut into small chunks, about 225 g/8 oz prepared weight

2 tbsp tomato purée
300 ml/10 fl oz vegetable stock
1–2 tsp hot paprika
few fresh sprigs of thyme
450 g/1 lb ripe tomatoes
soured cream and crusty bread, to serve

Vegetable Goulash

Put the sun-dried tomatoes in a small heatproof bowl, cover with almost boiling water and leave to soak for 15–20 minutes. Drain, reserving the soaking liquid. Meanwhile, rinse and drain the lentils, and put them in a saucepan with the cold water and bring to the boil. Reduce the heat, cover and simmer for 15 minutes. Drain and set aside.

Heat the oil in a large, heavy-based saucepan, with a tight-fitting lid, and cook the chillies, garlic and vegetables, stirring frequently, for 5–8 minutes until softened. Blend the tomato purée with a little of the stock in a jug and pour over the vegetable mixture, then add the remaining stock, lentils, the sun-dried tomatoes and their soaking liquid, and the paprika and thyme.

Bring to the boil, then reduce the heat, cover and simmer for 15 minutes. Add the fresh tomatoes and simmer for a further 15 minutes, or until the vegetables and lentils are tender. Serve topped with spoonfuls of soured cream, accompanied by crusty bread.

SERVES 4

1 aubergine, cut into 2.5-cm/1-inch slices
1 tbsp olive oil, plus extra for brushing
1 large red or yellow onion, finely chopped
2 red or yellow peppers, deseeded and finely chopped
3–4 garlic cloves, finely chopped or crushed

800 g/1 lb 12 oz canned chopped tomatoes
1 tbsp mild chilli powder
½ tsp ground cumin
½ tsp dried oregano
2 small courgettes, quartered lengthways and sliced
400 g/14 oz canned kidney beans, drained and rinsed

450 ml/16 fl oz water
1 tbsp tomato purée
6 spring onions, finely chopped
115 g/4 oz Cheddar cheese, grated
salt and pepper
crusty bread, to serve

Vegetable Chilli

Brush the aubergine slices on one side with olive oil. Heat half the oil in a large, heavy-based frying pan. Add the aubergine slices, oiled-side up, and cook over a medium heat for 5–6 minutes, or until browned on one side. Turn the slices over, cook on the other side until browned and transfer to a plate. Cut into bite-sized pieces and reserve.

Heat the remaining oil in a large saucepan over a medium heat. Add the chopped onion and peppers to the saucepan and cook, stirring occasionally, for 3–4 minutes, or until the onion is just softened, but not browned. Add the garlic and cook for a further 2–3 minutes, or until the onion just begins to colour.

Add the tomatoes, chilli powder, cumin and oregano. Season to taste with salt and pepper. Bring just to the boil, reduce the heat, cover and simmer gently for 15 minutes.

Add the sliced courgettes, aubergine pieces and kidney beans. Stir in the water and tomato purée. Return to the boil, then cover the saucepan and simmer for a further 45 minutes, or until the vegetables are tender. Taste and adjust the seasoning, if necessary.

Ladle into warmed bowls and top with spring onions and cheese. Serve with crusty bread.

SERVES 4

1 aubergine
225 g/8 oz turnips
350 g/12 oz new
   potatoes
225 g/8 oz cauliflower
225 g/8 oz button
   mushrooms
1 large onion
3 carrots
6 tbsp ghee or vegetable
   oil

2 garlic cloves, crushed
4 tsp chopped ginger
1–2 fresh green chillies,
   deseeded and
   chopped
1 tbsp paprika
2 tsp ground coriander
1 tbsp mild or medium
   curry powder
450 ml/16 fl oz vegetable
   stock

400 g/14 oz canned
   chopped tomatoes
1 green pepper,
   deseeded and sliced
1 tbsp cornflour
150 ml/5 fl oz coconut
   milk
salt
freshly cooked rice,
   to serve
fresh coriander sprigs,
   to garnish

Mixed Vegetable Curry

Cut the aubergine, turnips and potatoes into 1-cm/½-inch cubes. Break the cauliflower into small florets. Leave the mushrooms whole if small or slice them thickly, if preferred. Slice the onion and carrots.

Heat the ghee in a large saucepan over a low heat. Add the onion, turnips, potatoes and cauliflower and cook, stirring frequently, for 3 minutes.

Add the garlic, ginger, chilli, paprika, ground coriander and curry powder and cook, stirring constantly, for 1 minute.

Add the stock, tomatoes, aubergine and mushrooms and season to taste with salt. Cover and simmer, stirring occasionally, for 30 minutes, or until tender. Add the green pepper and carrots, cover and cook for a further 5 minutes.

Put the cornflour and coconut milk in a bowl, mix into a smooth paste and stir into the vegetable mixture. Simmer, stirring constantly, for 2 minutes. Taste and adjust the seasoning, if necessary. Transfer to serving bowls, garnish with coriander sprigs and serve immediately with freshly cooked rice.

SERVES 6

2 tbsp olive oil or
  vegetable oil
225 g/8 oz risotto rice
2 garlic cloves, crushed
1 onion, chopped
2 celery sticks, chopped
1 red pepper, deseeded
  and chopped
225 g/8 oz mushrooms,
  thinly sliced

1 tbsp chopped fresh
  oregano or 1 tsp dried
  oregano
1 litre/1¾ pints hot
  vegetable stock
55 g /2 oz sun-dried
  tomatoes in olive oil,
  drained and chopped
  (optional)

55 g/2 oz finely grated
  Parmesan cheese
salt and pepper
fresh flat-leaf parsley
  sprigs or bay leaves,
  to garnish

Parmesan Risotto with Mushrooms

Heat the oil in a deep saucepan. Add the rice and cook over a low heat, stirring constantly, for 2–3 minutes, until the grains are thoroughly coated in oil and translucent.

Add the garlic, onion, celery and red pepper and cook, stirring frequently, for 5 minutes. Add the mushrooms and cook for 3–4 minutes. Stir in the oregano.

Gradually add the hot stock, a ladle at a time. Stir constantly and add more liquid as the rice absorbs each addition. Increase the heat to medium so that the liquid bubbles. Cook for 20 minutes, or until all the liquid is absorbed and the rice is creamy. Add the sun-dried tomatoes, if using, 5 minutes before the end of the cooking time and season to taste with salt and pepper.

Remove the risotto from the heat and stir in half the Parmesan until it melts. Transfer the risotto to warmed bowls. Top with the remaining cheese, garnish with flat-leaf parsley and serve immediately.

SERVES 4–6

½ tsp saffron threads
2 tbsp hot water
6 tbsp olive oil
1 Spanish onion, sliced
3 garlic cloves, minced
1 red pepper, deseeded
    and sliced

1 orange pepper,
    deseeded and sliced
1 large aubergine, cubed
200 g/7 oz medium-grain
    paella rice
600 ml/1 pint vegetable
    stock
450 g/1 lb tomatoes,
    peeled and chopped

115 g/4 oz button
    mushrooms, sliced
115 g/4 oz French beans,
    halved
400 g/14 oz canned
    pinto beans
salt and pepper

Vegetarian Paella

Put the saffron threads and water in a small bowl or cup and leave to infuse for a few minutes.

Meanwhile, heat the oil in a paella pan or wide, shallow frying pan and cook the onion over a medium heat, stirring, for 2–3 minutes, or until softened. Add the garlic, peppers and aubergine and cook, stirring frequently, for 5 minutes.

Add the rice and cook, stirring constantly, for 1 minute, or until glossy and coated. Pour in the stock and add the tomatoes, saffron and its soaking water, and season to taste with salt and pepper. Bring to the boil, then reduce the heat and leave to simmer, shaking the frying pan frequently and stirring occasionally, for 15 minutes.

Stir in the mushrooms, French beans and pinto beans with their can juices. Cook for a further 10 minutes, then serve immediately.

SERVES 4-6

225 g/8 oz basmati rice
30 g/1 oz ghee or
   2 tbsp vegetable or
   groundnut oil
5 green cardamom pods,
   bruised

5 cloves
2 bay leaves
½ cinnamon stick
1 tsp fennel seeds
½ tsp black mustard
   seeds

450 ml/16 fl oz water
1½ tsp salt
2 tbsp chopped fresh
   coriander
pepper

Spiced Basmati Rice

Rinse the basmati rice in several changes of water until the water runs clear, then leave to soak for 30 minutes. Drain and set aside until ready to cook.

Melt the ghee in a flameproof casserole or large saucepan with a tight-fitting lid over a medium–high heat. Add the spices and stir for 30 seconds. Stir the rice into the casserole so the grains are coated with ghee. Stir in the water and salt and bring to the boil.

Reduce the heat to as low as possible and cover the casserole tightly. Simmer, without lifting the lid, for 8–10 minutes, until the grains are tender and all the liquid is absorbed.

Turn off the heat and use 2 forks to mix in the coriander. Adjust the seasoning, if necessary. Re-cover the pan and leave to stand for 5 minutes. Serve immediately.